MOUNTAINS AND CAVERNS

Mountains and Caverns

Selected Essays by

Alan Sillitoe

W. H. Allen · London
A division of Howard & Wyndham Ltd
1975

Printed and bound in Great Britain by
The Garden City Press Limited,
Letchworth, Hertfordshire SG6 1JS
for the Publishers, W. H. Allen & Co Ltd,
44 Hill Street, London W1X 8LB

ISBN 0 491 01834 7

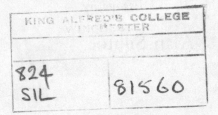

Contents

Acknowledgements

THE LONG PIECE—published here for the first time—contains information and comments from many lectures and interviews. The account of my first meeting with Robert Graves comes from an article printed in the *Shenandoah Review*.

EVACUATED is from *The Evacuees*, an anthology by B. S. Johnson published by Gollancz in 1968.

NATIONAL SERVICE is from another anthology by B. S. Johnson entitled *All Bull*, Allison & Busby, 1973.

MAPS was first given as a lecture to the Geography Faculty at Nebraska State University, Lincoln, Nebraska, USA, on October 1st 1974. Part of it was published in the *Geographical Magazine*, London, 1975.

POOR PEOPLE was published in *Anarchy* in April 1964.

DESTINY OF INSIGNIFICANCE is from *Mental Health*, Spring 1966.

SPORT AND NATIONALISM was given as a speech organised by the P.E.N. club in Cologne in 1972, as a counterweight to the Olympic Games which had just been held in Munich.

GOVERNMENT FORMS was originally entitled 'Why I don't like filling in government forms' and appeared in *The Times* on April 8th 1972.

THE WILD HORSE was part of a symposium on violence in the magazine *Twentieth Century* in the winter 1964/65 issue.

THROUGH THE TUNNEL was an essay written during a stay in Prague in August 1963. It was published in the *World Marxist Review* in January 1965, at which time it was deemed suitable.

ARNOLD BENNETT: THE MAN FROM THE NORTH is based on an introduction to the Pan Books editions of *Riceyman Steps* and *The Old Wives' Tale*, 1964.

CHE GUEVARA was written originally as an introduction to *Ernesto: A memoir of Che Guevara* by Hilda Gadea, W. H. Allen, 1963.

LAWRENCE AND DISTRICT is from a symposium on D. H. Lawrence edited by Stephen Spender and put out by Weidenfeld & Nicholson in 1972.

ROBERT TRESSELL was an introduction to the first paperback edition of *The Ragged Trousered Philanthropists* in Panther Books, in 1965.

MOUNTAINS AND CAVERNS was published early this year (1975) as part of an anthology by Frederic Raphael called *Bookmarks* (Jonathan Cape).

The Long Piece

I was born in 1928, on March 4th, under the sign of Pisces, in the front bedroom of a red-bricked council house on the further outskirts of Nottingham. We left the neighbourhood some months later, and though I lived a few miles from it during much of my life, I didn't see the house till I was over forty, while casually walking around the area one day. Otherwise it had had no interest for me.

My father worked at a tannery—or skinyard, as he called it—and I remember my mother taking my elder sister and me along Lenton Cut one Friday afternoon to meet him coming home with his wages. It was one of my first memories, and not unpleasant, because at that particular time my parents were reasonably content. My father took the two-pounds-odd from his wage-packet and slung the small brown envelope into the water. On turning my head I saw it floating like a miniature raft towards the depths of a nearby lock. It was the last wage-packet any of us saw till the war began in 1939.

A few weeks later my mother and her sister took me with them to Nazareth House at Lenton, to ask the nuns for bread. It was known in the neighbourhood that they occasionally had a surplus, and would give it out to first-comers.

From the beginning we children witnessed the dumb god-damn suffering of our parents, who were not able to do anything about what was happening to them—the eternal fate of such people everywhere. Bitterness was the only comfort available but because my father couldn't read or write, it lacked the subtle edge that might have led him to find some way out.

My first attitude towards my parents therefore was to feel sorry for them, and maybe this prevented me later from going through

9

the phase of adolescent rebellion that many children who have had it better seem to find necessary. How can you 'rebel' against a father whom you have seen in tears because he has been unable even to sell the power of his muscles and the sweat of his brow?

There were five children, and in some respects we were quite well looked after by the state. Without the dole for month after month we would have starved to death. We were able to go at eight in the morning, before starting school, to a 'dinner centre' for a breakfast of bread and butter, and hot, well-sugared cocoa; and again at midday for a hot meal of main course and pudding. During the morning in the classroom there was a free bottle of milk.

So while it was hell for the parents, it wasn't too bad for the children, except that the parents' suffering often harrowed the minds of the children. There was of course the low-keyed misery for the children of going through the winter with battered shoes that continually let the wet in—which was real enough. The music of rain spattering against the windows while we were warm and protected in the classroom lost some of its charm when the thought occurred to me that I would soon have to walk through it with saturated feet and no overcoat. My sister and I, maybe when we were eight or nine, went through a period of praying together in the hope that things would get better. We prayed to God though, never Jesus Christ, but since there was no improvement, it didn't last long.

I was favoured and helped by my grandparents. Grandfather Burton was employed as a blacksmith at Wollaton Pit a few miles outside Nottingham, shoeing ponies underground. There was work there for his sons also, but they preferred to travel to the Raleigh factory at Nottingham every day, for you only went down the pit and sweated at the face when you couldn't get a job anywhere else.

I spent most weekends and school holidays at their cottage, a mile or so in the country—walked alone to it over fields, through a green region that had somehow been left intact between slag heaps and colliery headstocks.

My grandfather was also illiterate, but there was a glass-fronted case of books in the parlour—Sunday school prizes which his eight children had brought home year after year throughout their growing up. I had never seen so many books in one house.

In school I was not one of the bright children. I liked the real learning that was to be done, but hated the discipline, and what seemed to me the hatred shown towards us by one or two teachers. There were the exceptions who, neither indifferent nor vicious, tried with genuine kindness to help us.

One of my first books came from a schoolmaster who gave away his personal collection before moving to another school. Its title was *History Day by Day*, a volume of nearly eight hundred pages, two being devoted to each day of the year.

Apart from events dealing with English history, other dates considered important concerned writers and artists. For example, under July 24th 1802 was recorded the birth of Alexandre Dumas. On one page was a brief account of his life, together with a list of his most famous works, and opposite was an extract from *The Count of Monte Cristo* the point where Edmond Dantès finally makes his escape from the dungeons of the Chateau d'If.

By browsing through such a compendium of fact, fiction, and brief biographies, I became familiar, though in a hotch-potch fashion, with both literature and history. It was a book exactly suited to my avid though shallow brain. Some extracts from novels were tantalising because they stopped skilfully at exciting points, so that I sought the book from the public library in order to finish it. My real education began, the painless and enjoyable sort that has not ended yet.

Les Misèrables, done as a serial play on the wireless, made such a strong impression that I saved up halfpenny by halfpenny to buy the book. I had already seen a copy in a neighbour's house, a Readers Library edition that was abridged, had yellow musty-smelling paper, and a hundred pages missing from the beginning. Nothing but the real thing would satisfy me, however, at the age of ten.

Exotic though it was in many ways, *Les Misèrables* seemed

relevant to me and life roundabout. No matter what is thought of that great novel now, it was the only adult book I read before the age of twenty. I haven't read it for many years, but chapter after chapter drew me out of my life and into the furnace, then pushed me back into life.

The figure of Jean Valjean, persecuted by the policeman Javert even after he had spent nineteen years in the galleys for stealing a loaf of bread to feed his sister and her starving children; the grim and unremitting tribulations of Fantine and her daughter Cosette; the unkillable and the ingenuous spirit of Gavroche the street urchin who reminded me vividly of one of my cousins and whose secret den was in the foot of the statue of an elephant; and later the revolutionary fighting in the streets of Paris during the 1830 insurrection, when Jean Valjean rescues one of the wounded fighters from the about-to-be-overrun barricades by carrying him through the sewers—all this was exciting and real, a saga I lived with almost till the time came for me to begin writing my own books.

In the darkness of an attic-room where we slept in one big bed (a room we went up into by a ladder and not a proper flight of stairs) I would tell the others tales before they went to sleep. I made up serial stories, as well as relating *Les Misèrables* or *The Count of Monte Cristo* time and time again, going from one gory episode to another by raking in my own additions when memory faltered or the brain got bored—until the voice of my fathered bellowed up that if we didn't go to sleep we'd get his fist.

When I was eleven my Grandmother Burton—may she rest in peace!—persuaded me to take a scholarship examination for a grammar school, which in those days was called a secondary school. She had noticed my preoccupation with the books in her parlour, though I had not been inspired to read them for they were of a religious or highly moral nature that did not appeal to me because I instinctively distrusted the sources from which they had come. I was also put off by the ornate and coloured labels inside the front covers, and in any case I was often too lazy to read.

But my grandmother said that if I passed the examination for the secondary school she would pay for my uniform and books by a loan from the Co-op—of which she had always been a member. This sounded a marvellous idea because I knew that at such places one was taught French. If I learned French the roads of the world would automatically open. Perhaps in some weird way I thought this because I had read two great novels which had been translated from that language.

A friend in the next street had a brother who taught him to count up to ten in French, and he passed this hot knowledge on to me. I bought a dictionary for sixpence, and attempted to render sentences from the newspaper into French simply by transposing words in the same order as in English. I soon realised that something was wrong, because I could never find the French for 'was' and 'be' and 'go'. Not knowing that such things as verbs existed was a rather serious impediment to going very far in my studies.

I failed the scholarship examination, as well as a chance to go to Nottingham High School the following year. This proved to me once and for all that I was not cut out for education.

II

After the war began my cousins, one by one, were called up into the Army. A few months later they came out again, one by one, and went home, and burned their uniforms in the bedroom grate. They then lived, without identity card or ration book, minus gas-mask or employment cards, and went on what was known in our family as 'night work'—sleeping and enjoying themselves by day, and burgling whatever was profitable at night.

As a boy of twelve I was aware of what was going on, and it wasn't long before I saw a half-column in the local newspaper which concerned my cousins. They had been caught, and sentenced to eighteen months in prison, so that within a year they were released and frog-marched back to the Army.

Then, after a spell in the glasshouse, one of them appeared like magic one morning at our breakfast table, wolfing bread and jam and swallowing tea. He was joined a few weeks later by his brother, also on the run again from the Army, and soon they were both back on 'night work'.

I was thirteen or fourteen, and wrote humorous doggerel, which I called verse. The idea came into my head that perhaps one day I would write novels set in the sort of life that was going on around me. My instinct told me that the most interesting thing I could delve into would be the adventures of my marauding cousins.

The enormity and importance of this writing task so impressed me that I bought a large limp-covered notebook in order to begin a dossier on every member of the family, but mostly my cousins. I noted their age, weight, height, colour of hair, where born and what worn, as well as address when they had one. Then I inscribed sketches of their past lives and brief Army careers, and entered accounts of their robberies and escapades—which included the date, time, and address of particular shops and offices broken into.

They would visit us at breakfast—at knocking off time, that is—and regale us with stories from their blackout labours, such crucial details appearing sooner in my notebook than in the local newspaper when they were finally caught. I intended storing this raw material —which seemed unique because nobody but me could have it at such an early stage, except perhaps the police, and even they did not have both sides of the story—so as to write a long novel.

But one day when I was at school my mother went through my things, found the book, and read it. No sooner was I in the door that afternoon than she clouted me over the head, and told me I should have more sense: 'What the bloody hell do you think you're doing, writing things like that? Do you want to get us all chucked in jail?'

I told her it was for my novel, but she took no notice, and threw my first literary effort into the flames. I decided in future to keep things in my head.

Undaunted, I went to the public library, and took out a book on how to make a career as a writer. The first sentence went something like: 'If you are reading these words without moving your lips you too can become a writer.'

Well, I *wasn't* moving my lips, and then the author of that work went on to say that the first thing necessary (apart from pen and paper) was a typewriter, in order that novels and stories could be sent off to publishers in a presentable form.

When my cousins came to visit us a few days later I quietly put the proposal to them that on next breaking into the appropriate premises they nick one for me. I would pay them back at two shillings a week when I started work. If I was lucky, I told myself, I could settle my debt with a lump sum when I got my first big fee for a novel. I kept a sly face, and did not let on that the substance of such a project would be culled out of their adventures.

They generously waived aside my business-like proposal, and said I could have one for nothing. Perhaps my mother had mentioned my secret ambition, and they were tickled at the idea of having their own biographer at some future date. Week after week I was waiting for a typewriter, but somehow they were never able to bring one. I imagine they found more portable things for the taking, and in any case were astute enough to see they might land me in trouble if the police ever thought to search our house and found one there.

In spite of my hope of getting a novel published at thirteen—or fourteen at the latest—I forgot all about it till I was twenty because I went to work. From the dream-world of thinking I could write a book, to the realistic life in which I and the Seaton family lived, was not such a big gap, and though it had widened considerably, I could still vaguely feel that a time would come in the future when it might not be difficult to span it again.

I didn't feel any immense sense of liberation from school, nor did I experience a shock on entering the 'savage' industrial world. It was rather with a sense of wonder and adventure that I went into it. I didn't particularly want to go, but I was resigned to my spirit getting bumped about a bit—in this traditional, incontrovertible necessity.

When I entered that marvellous brick hall with its high dark windows, and gangwayed forest of intricate and awe-inspiring machines, I knew I had left something behind which I could never rejoin. I grew to like such daily life after the first few weeks of familiarisation—in spite of the noise, and the metallic tang of shaved steel and brass. At that age I could have become anything—soldier, sailor, mechanic, baker, tailor—if I had been thrust into it. Underneath my reluctance to change was enough resilience to get me over any hurdles, as well as sufficient numbness not to notice what was happening.

Nevertheless it was difficult to accustom myself to it, especially to the number of minor physical knocks which digits, arms, eyes and feet took from wayward drills, flying tinders and sharp corners. A couple of dreamy minutes were paid for by a sudden gash at the fingertop, or a bus trip to the Infirmary in town with a hand over the eye.

But there were diversions, and consolations. One became interested in going out with girls, and having a good time on the three or four shillings a week pocket money given back from the wage packet. At night the blackout was complete, and cloaked many a courtship that came to nothing, and heightened many that ought not to have started.

There was no factory in England, it seemed, which was not turning out goods to be used directly in the war against Germany. One of the jobs I took to was that of capstan-lathe operator. It was not skilled work. Anyone could become adept after a few days. But I liked the job because it was repetitive. My thoughts had freedom while my hands went through the six operations without thinking. A thousand times a day I set the bar, spun back the turret, pushed in the chamfer, forced the drill, and worked two cutting blades till the simple brass hexagonal nut fell into my right hand and was thrown into a tin. In two years I suppose I made six hundred thousand, which were sent to Rolls Royce at Derby for use in Spitfire and bomber engines.

I was a perfectly integrated workman by the time I was sixteen, and considered myself adult enough to formulate rough thoughts on politics. I found it impossible to work in a factory without believing that socialism was the ultimate solution for all life on this planet—easy for an impressionable youth to assume such a thing in wartime because there actually did seem to be a feeling of equality, and an air of common purpose about life.

On the other hand perhaps I thought socialism so attractive because I hoped that, if ever it came about, it might get everyone else in the country doing the same sort of labour, and then I wouldn't have to spend so long on it myself. It sounds plausible, yet it wasn't true, because there was no bitterness in my beliefs. And I liked working in a factory. It seemed only just that the riches produced by such arduous work should be distributed also among those who made them.

Yet while I fervently believed in the economic benefits of social-ism, it was not easy, due perhaps to my lack of experience and imagination, to see people in 'class' terms. The labels 'working class' and 'middle class' had little reality for me because I had contact only with individual people. I suppose I was so blindly embedded in my own narrow life of family, factory and group, that I could not see beyond, in spite of evidence from books and cinema, and my juvenile dabbling with the simple but attractive ideas of com-munism. I had no particular ambition to get away from the life I led—though I knew I would have to go into the Air Force at eighteen. I also knew that ever since I was conscious as a child my one great desire had been to travel, to get out of the country I was born into. We are made up of dozens of large fragments, which are continually changing their situations and alliances.

I switched jobs every year or so, and at sixteen worked at a small engineering firm which employed no more than thirty people. The owner came in wearing overalls like his workmen at eight every morning, and he'd spend the day testing work at his own bench with special lighting, or talking with his toolsetters about the jobs to be done. Or he would turn some piece of his own making on a large centre-lathe outside the 'office' door, and a stranger coming in would see only a workman like the rest of us. So I couldn't regard him as 'middle class' or even very different from myself. He owned the 'factory', but was assessed individually and not as a member of a 'class'. We had to be wary, however, because he was the boss after all; but no one was ever in awe of him.

The war was on, and there was work for everybody. We were rationed for food, but I never heard anyone complain about lack of it. Life had one particular end in view, which was the defeat of Germany and Nazism—of which we were all aware in varying degrees.

The factory was built by a railway embankment, and during June 1944 I remember looking up in my dinner hour and seeing trains whose khaki-coloured carriages were marked by large red crosses, carrying wounded back from Normandy. It was a reminder perhaps that class warfare could not be indulged in at such a time. The lesson that 'politics is the art of the possible' is often hard enough to learn, but in wartime it was more or less realised: its catastrophic failure having already set the conflict spinning in the first place.

III

I am occasionally asked how it was that I became a writer, and I have never been able to answer that question, either to my own or to anybody else's satisfaction. Who cares? Perhaps the question is more interesting than any possible answer. The implication is that if I had been to secondary or grammar school, and university, there would have been no reason to ask. I suppose it was natural that, because I had not been educated beyond the age of fourteen, they wanted to know how I had become literate—which is all that being a writer is. Maybe it would have been equally strange if I'd turned into a dentist or a lawyer, but as far as I am concerned it would have been stranger still if, university or no, I had not turned into a writer. There was nothing else I could have done. All mysteries are wrapped up in the complexities of a simple explanation.

At eighteen I entered the Air Force and was trained as a wireless operator/teleprinter operator. I went to Malaya for eighteen months, during which time the communist guerrillas began an insurrection against the British occupying power of which I, unwittingly, was a part. But I was due to be discharged from military service, and travelled back from Singapore to a demobilisation camp in England.

My friends and I were called in alphabetically to have an X-ray, so that it could be proved we were going out as physically fit as when we came in. This being so, we would then be sent home with sufficient back pay to have a good time. The question as to what work I would do after demob, that had bothered me on the troopship *Dunera* the whole eight thousand miles back, no longer seemed important. The future would take care of itself, as long as I *got out*. I was simply looking forward to seeing my family again, and if afterwards I had to get a job in some factory or other, what of it? It was no more than I'd been used to.

After my X-ray, instead of being given money and a railway warrant, I was asked back into the medical office. The MO wasn't happy—he said—about my X-ray. In fact it was not very good at all, with so many black and pitted marks down the left side, and a few beginning to appear on the right. 'You have tuberculosis, I'm sorry to say. You'll have to go into hospital for treatment.'

'How long will it take to cure?' I wanted to know, choking on my words as I tried to take in what exactly he meant.

There would be no cure. 'Not just like that, at any rate,' was his tactful reply. 'You may be in hospital for one year, perhaps two. It's hard to say till we've done more tests. You'll have to lie on your back for a goodly length of time, that's all I can tell you at the moment.'

I recalled that when I first went into the senior school at the age of eleven a much bigger boy already there pinned me against the wall and with a jeering bellow said: 'You're going to get consumption!' He wasn't dangerous, and it didn't mean much because he said it to everyone. I was told that his sister had died of it two years before. My aunt's boy-friend, who used to give me huge cigarette cards from his packets of twenty Players, died of it. A girl-friend's father also, as well as a friend's mother, and somebody's sister up the street. It must have been the biggest killer in the thirties, and on the Home Front during the war, when more than twice as many people died from it as from air raids. When I copped it people were dying at the rate of twenty-five thousand a year: it was almost like being told today that you have cancer. We called it consumption, and in my moments of nightmare I'd often dreaded getting it.

I had led an active life, and this was a shattering blow. I'd been ill for months already, but hadn't really noticed it. Certainly, I'd become thin, but that had seemed nothing out of the ordinary. My body was something I'd never thought about. It was indestructible. There was no amount of walking or swimming or labouring it couldn't do. But obviously there was. Sooner or later you have to pay for living in a state of oblivion.

The idea of spending one or two years in hospital struck me as so appalling that for a long time I was in a state of shock. If I'd been hit by a bullet I'd have been happier about it, but to go down with a disease such as this seemed an ineradicable disgrace.

Immediately after the X-ray I was given ten days' sick leave. My family and friends in Nottingham said how fit I looked, how slim and tanned after my time abroad. One of my aunts, however, the mother of my marauding cousins, said I looked like 'death warmed up'.

Before going back for the long stretch I tried to tell my father what I'd got, mumbling euphemisms when we were alone in the pub one night, unable to say the dreaded word directly, so that he thought I was trying to tell him I'd got a dose of syphilis from my sojourn in those foreign and tropical parts. He patted me on the back and said that it happened to the best of them, and that no doubt I'd soon get over it. 'It's nowt ter worry yersen about, my lad. They cure owt nowadays.'

To my mother I said I'd picked up some vague fever in Malaya which would put me in hospital for a time, so no one was unduly worried.

I returned to Lytham St Anne's for blood, sputum and further X-ray tests, which all proved positive, and to wait and see which hospital I would go to. I stayed three weeks in a small ward on my own. It was like being in solitary confinement, for I saw no one except the orderly who brought in my food. I needed no medical looking-after, but the uncertainty and isolation put me in a state near to madness. Usually there would have been a few other patients in the ward awaiting transfer, but at this time I was the only one.

I wrote an account of a trip half a dozen of us had done in June 1948, an attempt to climb Gunong Jerai (in Kedah State) as a practice jungle-rescue exercise. It had happened only three months before, yet seemed centuries ago. The six days and nights in all-engulfing forest were remembered from my bed as an ideal state of existence. To spend hours climbing and crawling through rotting, snake-infested forest with forty pounds of tinned food on my back as well as rifle, ammunition, mosquito net and blanket, water-bottle and kukri, and a haversack containing maps and notebook—and a prismatic compass, because I was the self-styled navigator of the expedition, having enlarged and copied maps of the area before setting out—was a state of perfection to look back on now that I was cooped up as an invalid in this nondescript camp in northern England.

I'd longed to be back in England, but not to this, by God. Fixing our position one morning in the jungle-clearing, by compass bearings on two nearby peaks, I found (after duly allowing for magnetic variation and grid differences) that we had progressed only 1,300 yards in ten hard hours. But it was real, something tangible to fight and struggle against.

I wrote my thirty-page narrative, a day by day account of a failed attempt to climb a four thousand-foot mountain—a pedestrian composition because I did not know how to exploit the full colour of the situation and so make it real to anyone who might read it.

Yet the diversity of the two existences opened me up to this colossal and perhaps salutary shock. An end had to be found to a certain part of my life, and it could be that there was no better way of doing it. The schizoid pattern imprinted itself. A dull burning took place. A light went out, and took a long time to come fully on again. I can find no other words, and would have used none better at the actual time—if I had been able to drum up any at all. The course of a life changes only because the life itself does not want to end. It has no intention of doing so, even when it has come to the fall from an enormous precipice. One somehow finds a way out.

I wanted to die in order to get away from the problem, yet it was the need to live which made the illness so hard to bear. And it had to be borne silently. One could not complain, or tell anyone about it during those first weeks of oblivion. When I was with others of the same age with the same disease, it grew to matter much less.

Not actually feeling ill gave paranoia a clear field to rove in. I wondered if some grim mistake had not been made, whether a series of X-rays hadn't got mixed up. I turned myself into the victim of an enormous hoax, a paranoiac stooge. Any day now, I thought, one of the medical officers will walk up the ward waving my X-ray and laughing in an embarrassed way as he explains that a name got mixed up, a shadow falsely read, and that I'm really as fit as . . .

Yet I knew my illness was real. I could no longer deny it to myself. I'd been losing weight for months in Malaya, even when cutting my way through the jungle and feeling so energetic and healthy—a clear symptom of the disease. It made you feel good. You could get high on it—after a good cough. Yet I still thought it ridiculous to be on my back for eighteen months for such a stupid reason.

I sent my jungle story to a friend in Nottingham, who kindly got his secretary to type it for me, and seeing it in such a form made it look so clear and close to print, double-spaced and on thick paper. that I was both pleased and bemused by it, and did not notice the naïvety and clumsiness of my first piece of writing. In a way it was almost as important to me as my first published work.

When I went to Swindon, on my way to the RAF hospital at Wroughton, I walked out of the station and was confronted by a coffin with a flag over it being unloaded from an RAF lorry before being put on a train. I asked the driver what the person had died of, and was told he'd been a patient at the hospital who had coughed his last. I was in uniform, so he asked if I wanted a lift back, not realising I was going there as a patient. I turned down his kind offer, preferring to walk around the town for some time.

I went into the widening desert of my brain, and lay in bed day after day feeling sorry for myself in order to stay sane. I opened the Bible that had been given to me at school and jabbed my finger on a random verse which fell appropriately on the third chapter of Lamentations: 'To subvert a man in his cause, the Lord approveth not.' It seemed meaningless, so I read Genesis and half of Exodus till an orderly brought in my supper.

As the weeks went by it came home to me more and more what having tuberculosis meant. I had become a deficient person, an invalid who would no longer be any use to himself or others, someone who could not get work in a factory because he was eternally ill, who would have this terrible fact written into his records for the rest of his life whenever he needed to change his job, and who no girl would want to know for fear of contagion. 'All days wherein the plague shall be in him he shall be defiled; he is unclean: he shall dwell alone; without the camp shall his habitation be.'

While still in Malaya I'd thought that maybe I would do a course at a radio school when I got out, and take a PMG Radio Operator's Certificate so as to find a job in the Merchant Navy. That was now out of the question. A friend I met more than ten years afterwards reminded me that in Malaya I'd even considered going into the Canadian Air Force as a radio operator—while I still assumed it was possible.

At twenty years of age the power of self-pity is strong, a form of madness which I worked through from beginning to end—without anyone knowing about it. It was like dying and being born again. But within the inner light of this psychic explosion another education was beginning, the real one, for I was reading all the books I could get my hands on, reaching out avidly for them when the trolley was pushed up to my bed two or three times a week.

I had hardly read any adult matter before, and now a great and prolonged feast began. Until then the sort of everyday speech I used and heard was in no way connected with books, but now I started to understand literary language—literature, if you like—for the first time.

One of my lungs was collapsed, which was no great pain or discomfort, but while quietly lying there I read, among other things, translations from the Greek and Latin classics, and as much English poetry as I could find. An old school edition of some Wordsworth poems had a section at the back on prosody—a word and subject I'd never heard of before. In a week I had taken it in, and then sent off for Egerton Smith's classic text-book on the matter.

I also began to write, so impressed was I with what I read. In Malaya I'd written odd poems and scraps of prose—generally concerned with the beauties of the scenery—to pass away the fourteen-hour shifts in my radio hut at the end of the runway.

But in Wroughton Hospital I wrote dozens of poems in empty wireless logbooks, and filled exercise jotters with sketches and bits of description, some of which turned into fragments for future novels and stories. Maybe I began this feverish bout of urgent writing to try and bring the true significance of this illness closer to me. This is as good an excuse as any, I suppose. In order to survive I had to try and explain to myself what this situation meant—a dramatic way of putting it perhaps, but I believe that at twenty I was a simpler person than I am now.

The life-saving story of that jungle mountain climb (which was no doubt what helped to speed me to this hospital bed) became, after numerous rewritings and shifting around, a couple of chapters in *Key to the Door* which was published thirteen years later.

A bad illness did have advantages, though it was difficult to think so at the time. They were perhaps too profound to be noticed.

IV

The events which a writer sees in his life as important may seem irrelevant to other people. Probably the most vital things happened to him before he even wrote his first few pages, and meant more to him than anything he will ever write.

It needed ten years to get a book published, so that when it did happen it came as no surprise. I had not gone through three years of university training on how to write essays or vivisect poems. If I had, the composition of some pastiche, with a dash of cynicism and a peppering of false worldliness, plus the unthinking acceptance of everything that traditional society stands for, might have brought the date much closer. I wasn't made that way. I didn't know any language apart from English—and that not very well. I could think only as fast as my slow-moving pen could write. It's not much different now—as far as logic is concerned. Essays and articles are still hard to get down: to connect one thought to another with ease and polish, not only to think of something to say but to develop an argument as well, to dominate the prose of cause and effect in an intelligent manner—makes me sweat blood.

The first draft of my first novel, written when I was twenty-two, was over four hundred pages long, and took seventeen days to write.

The title *By What Road* was part of a line from the Bhagavad Gita translated by Sir Edwin Arnold. With the temerity of youthful unconsciousness I sent the typescript to Eyre and Spottiswoode, who had announced a literary competition for new novels. It came back without comment. As a story it was chaotic. I believe everybody died in the end—or nearly everybody. All I have left is the handwritten copy, which I haven't dared to read since.

When my brother came to visit me in Majorca some years later I had so few clothes that he left me his black teddy-boy suit with drainpipe trousers, and I gave him the manuscript of this primal work as a poor form of compensation. Later still, when I began to be published, I bought it back for fifty pounds.

What the novel lacked in technique it made up for in energy and verbosity, an unequal balance that gave it a naïve and ludicrous aspect. I used ten adjectives where one would do, employed the same word many times on one page, repeated myself, started the hero with brown eyes and fair hair, and changed these—quite unknowingly—to fair eyes and brown hair by the fortieth page. I lost track of the plot: someone killed stone dead early on by a lorry turned up alive and kicking on page 100. It was a vainglorious mish-mash of Dostoevsky, D. H. Lawrence and Aldous Huxley— to name but a few. It was not related to life in any way, yet I naturally considered it a work that had a chance of being published.

Many of the poems and stories I wrote at this time were burned a year or so later, for it soon seemed to me that the first stage in the development of a writer, who could just about spell properly by the time he came to write his first novel, was that he becomes irresponsibly handy with a box of matches.

One of the first complete stories I wrote was called 'Uncle Ernest', and I sent it to the editor of every English magazine I knew of, but it was not published for seven years, when it came out in *The Loneliness of the Long-Distance Runner* collection, and was greatly praised.

While living at home I had a story published in the *Nottinghamshire Weekly Guardian*, for which I got one pound ten shillings. It was called 'No Shot in the Dark'—another incident from Malaya, and reprinted only in my German publisher's magazine twenty years later. Otherwise it was ploughed like so much else into my third novel *Key to the Door*.

In the autumn of 1950, in a friend's secondhand bookshop, I met a nineteen-year-old American girl who was also a writer and poet, named Ruth Fainlight. In a magazine we saw an advertisement for an unfurnished house to let near the south coast of France for forty-eight pounds a year. Because I had tuberculosis, which seemed in no way to frighten her, we decided it would be good to live in a more southern place. From being a deadweight on society I had become a romantic.

We collected the money to pay a quarter's rent in advance, as well as the train fare down and enough for a sparse living when we got there. On my passport I wrote my occupation as 'writer'—a piece of bare-faced hope that gave me a sense of identity, at a time when I certainly needed one.

Since I'd caught TB in the Air Force I came into a pension of three pounds a week, and on this we intended to live. We expected to stay away from England for six months, but didn't get back for six years.

v

One wet January morning in 1952 we went on to the Newhaven–Dieppe boat with a great deal of shabby-looking luggage—and a ginger female cat we couldn't bear to leave behind, chewing a raw herring in a specially made box. The boat went out of a gap in the breakwater and entered a violent sea, where the Atlantic's savage waves were doing their best to stuff England up the Skaggerak.

We'd eaten a British Railways wonder lunch before the boat left harbour, which self-indulgence I think was a pity, looking back on it, for two reasons, one being that it was a waste of food, and the other because I didn't have the pleasure of seeing the grey cliffs recede in the appropriate poetic vision which an English writer usually has when he first heads for the mainland—since I was ill the whole four hours across. I have not been seasick since, and many years have passed, though I have been in seas even worse. But there was a special reason for it then, there being a lot of England I had to get rid of before I could begin my new life as a writer.

Twenty-four hours later we were in the blue sky and sunshine of southern France. It was a marvellous awakening. The only one comparable was when I first left England on a troopship for the East, when after ten days out I walked up the companionway one morning to see palm trees and camels on the banks of the Suez Canal. The Mediterranean had been grey from end to end, stormy and bleak, and this unexpected vision almost blinded me. Now, I had come to France with someone I loved, and that made all the difference.

Leaving most of our luggage at the station in Menton we walked the couple of kilometres beyond the town, then a hundred metres up a hill, to find the house we were to live in. To cut off the endless curves of the cart road we ascended by hundreds of narrow stone steps, with a low wall on either side, going between mimosa, eucalyptus, pine and arbutus trees. We had a suitcase each, and so went up slowly. The mimosa was cold, yellow and abundant, its odour filling the air. Even today I can never see or smell it without being taken vividly back to the first climb of those stone steps of the Cernuschi estate.

During the afternoon I borrowed a handcart from the concierge and pushed it across town to the station, where I loaded our luggage and heaved it back up the hairpin bends to the house.

It was in an olive grove, with five cold and empty rooms, only one of which had electricity—a single bare low-powered light-bulb hanging from the ceiling. Cooking was to be done in a fireplace, and water fetched from a pump in front of the villa. When we washed at it, and drew the first buckets and bowls of the morning, half a dozen small green frogs would come tumbling with it out of the iron spout, then go hopping away across the gravel, waiting among the bushes till we had done before making back for the pump again. Ruth wrote a poem about it.

Fuel for the fire was chopped from a mimosa grove nearby, and we ripped off huge sheets of eucalyptus bark for kindling. In short, it was an ideal life for someone who had the use of only one lung. We couldn't afford to buy much more than bread, fruit, vegetables and olive oil, with the occasional egg or fish thrown in.

The property surrounded an old Italian villa, and I think that in more prosperous days our house had belonged to the coachman. The proprietor was coming down by car from London with his English wife, and was supposed to arrive at the same time as us so that, as promised, he could sell us a few bits of old furniture stored in their attic. But his wife became ill, and it was a fortnight before they got to Menton, so we had to push cases and trunks together

28

to make a bed, and sling a hammock we'd fortunately brought from England.

The third morning we woke to see snow on the ground, and for weeks it was bitterly cold, or damp from heavy rain. Many people in the area were killed by floods and landslides. But by May the weather began to clear.

It was a beautifully secluded house, and a good atmosphere to work in. Ruth wrote many stories and poems. I turned out two more novels. *Saturday Night and Sunday Morning* really began there, because I did one chapter as a short story which was later incorporated into it.

We tried to place our bits and pieces by sending them to London when we could afford the postage, but neither publishers nor magazine editors showed interest—except that I had two short travel articles in the *Nottinghamshire Weekly Guardian*, and got a few pounds for a story called 'The Match' from a French newspaper, while a story of Ruth's was published in the *Jewish Monthly*.

We cooked, washed our clothes in the estate wash-house when nobody was there, wrote, climbed the hillsides, and shopped in Italy a few miles away because it was marginally cheaper. We wore unironed clothes, drank no wine or coffee, cut each other's hair when it got too long, and queued for stale bread with the poor on Monday.

Ruth's aunt posted food parcels from America, and a few dollars now and again. My sister in Nottingham occasionally sent a package of surplus powdered milk which was left over from feeding her children. By counting every franc spent, it was possible to manage, but occasionally, while waiting for my pension to come through, we'd have to fend a few days on potatoes, and what fruit we could plunder from the estate.

There was a great feeling of isolation, of having escaped, of being together, of having done the right thing. It was difficult to think about anyone except ourselves, of ought but surviving from day to day, and writing. There were great pleasures, at the same time, in the beautiful surroundings, the pleasant nearby town, the sea to the south and the wall of mountains to the north.

We had brought a few books, and could borrow from an English library in town—a vital help. I visited a doctor every fortnight to get my chest pumped with air so as to keep my lung down and at rest. Coming back up the hill after one of these sessions was a slower process than usual.

VI

After a year in France we went to Majorca where, we were told by friends, living was cheaper. We settled in the town of Soller, a tolerant and good-natured place, for whose hospitality I shall always be grateful, because we worked peacefully and consistently there for five years.

I was alone for a time, while Ruth was in England, so I stayed at the house of John Tarr, who'd published books on handwriting and calligraphy after an early retirement from the Monotype Corporation. He lived, with his wife, in a draughty old villa near the port, and the winter was long and rainy, weeks of wet and wind mouldering everything.

I began to write a book about Majorca called 'A Stay of Some Time' (not published) which I worked on for the next few years, adding chapters as I got to know more about the island. The title was a quotation from *Spain and Portugal* by Karl Baedeker—I never travelled without having one of his handbooks with me.

I'd heard that Robert Graves also lived on the island, so I sent him some of my poems, and he wrote back asking me to come over to Deyá one Sunday and have tea. On the first fine weekend of spring I borrowed a bicycle and pedalled up the mountain road. Trees in the valley were heavy with lemons and oranges, perfuming the route for much of the way up, and when its last half-dozen loops reached the col I was rewarded by a wide horizon of the Balearic Sea. Olive groves and pine trees descended to black giantesque rocks by the shore, holding back a hypnotic, gently heaving sheet of blue.

When I'd had my fill of it I set off downhill, and went almost to Deyá without pedalling.

The house was easy to find— a grey structure by an elbow of road before the village. I left my bicycle on the garden path, and walked to the back door that was shielded by a hanging curtain of fine steel chain. No one was in sight. Green shoots showed on the grapevine already, and an assortment of broken toys was strewn around the door: bows and arrows, a dancing shoe, a satchel, and a boy's bicycle leaning against the wall.

'Anybody in?' I called. The movement of a chair sounded, then footsteps, and two hands parted the chain curtain. Graves stood, a pair of scissors in one hand and a jug in the other, towering above me—it seemed—so I stepped back to make the difference in our heights less pronounced. He looked quizzical, as if he might have seen me somewhere before and couldn't quite place me.

I told him my name, adding that I lived in Soller, and had written to him. He thought for a moment, then said: 'I received your letter.' He left the jug on the kitchen table, crossed the step and came outside: 'I'm going to pick some lemons for lemonade. How did you get from Soller?'

'By bicycle. I'll give you a hand if you like.'

We went into the garden, tugging fruit from trees and filling a straw basket. 'Some of your poems are good,' he said, still looking at me as if waiting for some sort of recognition. 'At least you end them well. So many people get off to a good start, then fizzle out half-way through.' He was a big man, with grizzled hair, a broken nose (from boxing, he told me), full lips, a vigorous head; he wore sandals, blue jeans, and a brown open-necked shirt—a well-built middle-aged sixty.

The living-room windows overlooked the sea. He poured two glasses of lemonade and sat at the large table covered with books and papers, signing a limited edition of his poems, a light labour that enabled us to talk through the scratching of his signature.

'There are no holidays for a writer,' he said, 'especially when he has a large family.'

'I find it impossible to work all the time.'

'So did I once, but it became a habit. Then it's not so difficult.' He set the sheets around him to dry. I relaxed while questions and answers crossed the table at the lazy rate of Sunday afternoon. I found his remarks about my poetry encouraging, but said that so far none had been published.

'That doesn't matter, as long as you keep writing them.' We talked about the various ways in which Ulysses and Telemachus were said to have died—the theme of one of my poems. 'Telemachus,' he told me (he was then working on *The Greek Myths*) 'was banned from Ithaca by Odysseus, who had been warned that his son would kill him—but it turned out to be another son, Telegonus. In the end Telemachus married Circe,' he smiled. 'Wasn't that strange?'

We went outside again. A few goat bells sounded lazily among the terraces, and nothing else, silence, solitude, as far down as the sea and beyond. 'What part of England do you come from?'

Nottingham: I hadn't seen it for some time, and the word came like a shock, bringing a sudden clear vision of packed streets and factory chimneys, of tar melting between cobblestones in summer, of riotous public houses on Saturday night.

'I've some pleasant memories of it,' he said, 'though I've never actually been there. When we were poor—after the Great War—I received a cheque for a hundred pounds from a Nottingham manufacturer. It was Christmas, and I gave the postman my last shilling as I took the letter. The man said in it that he didn't think poets should starve, and that he hoped the enclosed would help me. Another time I was to go before a medical reassessment board for my pension, and the railway warrant was made out to Nottingham by mistake. I was so ill by the time I got to my real destination that the pension was kept on! I'm sure Nottingham's a town worth writing about, if you're thinking of doing a novel.'

Walking slowly along the road, he asked if I knew anything about the Nottingham habit where a girl, saying a loud goodbye to a boy-friend late at night after her parents had gone to bed, slams the house door with him still on the inside. Of course I knew about it. I said it still went on, and remembered this when I wrote *Saturday Night and Sunday Morning.*

Back in the house, sitting down over a drink, Graves still signing his poems, he asked what university I'd been to. 'I didn't go to any,' I told him. 'I left school early.'

'So did I, I left to go to the Great War.' Poverty was an important topic, and he asked how I was managing to live in Majorca. I told him I had a pension, having been invalided out of the Air Force. This led to T. E. Lawrence and *The Mint*. Lawrence, he said, had been kind to poets, and in the twenties had given him a first edition of *The Seven Pillars of Wisdom*, which he had been able to sell for three hundred pounds.

His wife came back with the children, and the table was cleared for tea. During the commotion Graves looked at me again and suddenly began sorting through a heap of papers on the window-sill. He took one out and held it up, then passed it to his wife: 'Who does this remind you of?' Both thought it resembled me—an engraving of Ludowick Muggleton, an eighteenth-century journey-man-preacher who started the sect of Muggletonians in the North of England, said to be still flourishing up to fifty years ago. 'I knew you reminded me of someone as soon as I saw you,' Graves said, pleased at having solved the puzzle.

We sat for some time drinking fiery Spanish brandy that later helped me on my way back to Soller—flying around the hairpin bends with more speed than wisdom.

VII

Ruth and I became good friends with Robert Graves. Apart from liking his poems and novels, I also agreed with his uncompromising attitude to critics, and his avoidance of literary fashions—views I discovered after long talks with him. By keeping to his high standards, he could afford not to give a damn for any malformed opinion about his work. And I myself have always lived by the

33

words of Tolstoy's advice to Maxim Gorki: 'Don't let anyone influence you, fear no one, and then you'll be all right.'

This doesn't mean that one shouldn't listen to friends, and after reading one of my novels—a fantasy story—Graves said to me: 'I like it, but why don't you write a book set in Nottingham, which is something you know about?' I answered that I might try it one day, and then appeared to forget the advice.

It was good to be away from England because I didn't have people nagging and sniping at me to get a job, and wondering why I was idling around year after year. Though I still got my pension, I felt as fit as I'd ever been.

A favourite spring and summer excursion was to the monastery at Lluch which, though only sixteen kilometres direct, was double that distance by foot path and muletrack, and meant a climb from sea level to over two thousand feet. Such treks over rough country were good, ropesoled sandals on the feet, a straw hat on the head, and a long-handled food basket holding sausage, olives and bread slung from the shoulder. We would return to Soller the following day, after a night in a cell at the monastery—where the good monks never thought to ask for our marriage lines!

Six years out of England was a long time, and after a while one even forgot the need ever to get back to it. The whole decade from twenty years to thirty years of age was a long time to be 'doing nothing', though I wrote seven novels before *Saturday Night and Sunday Morning*.

It was also good to be in a place where English wasn't the tongue spoken, because my own language then became sharper for being isolated. I learned Spanish, enough of the Majorcan dialect to translate folk songs, and sufficient French to speak it roughly and read it well. After a while it became apparent that such knowledge was a good way of getting at the roots of my own language— something which is essential for a writer.

We shifted from one house or flat to another, furnished places that never cost more than a pound a week. We lived without newspapers or magazines, and were culturally severed from England. The magazines we read, the people we met, the books we got hold of, came from Paris or New York or San Francisco, places which at that time exuded a more interesting and energetic literary influence than the country we had left.

In winter, when the island was clothed in rain and cloud for weeks at a time (much as George Sand had described it over a hundred years before) we read aloud to each other, a few chapters every evening. One book was *The Confessions of an English Opium Eater* by de Quincey, an exercise which gave me a feeling for the language that I might not have got either from reading it to myself, or by listening to it. The rhythm of its style became dramatically and pleasurably apparent, revealing a richness I must strive for in my own prose, if it were to be effective.

I saw it would be useful to read my stories and chapters in this way, to make sure they had both the fluidity and clarity of good English. It was easier to pick out the number of repetitions on a page, and to spot unnecessary words. Some might be there because I had discovered them that day in the dictionary or thesaurus. Tautologies I scratched out. I got rid of clichés and false phrases, or any other rubbish that didn't have much meaning to it. I eliminated items which were implied rather than stated. To be plain, poetic, and profound was extremely difficult, but it was a step forward to know that it had to be attempted, and to see possible ways to do it. I was gaining confidence in what I was trying to say, starting to use the techniques of poetry, which seemed the only way to write good prose.

Good English is clear English. I had to discover this before I could inject into it whatever personal style I had. Then I could make what I was writing echo my own inner voice, the way my thoughts spoke to me when I did not have a pen in my hand. This is elementary and simple, but for me it was like coming out of a wilderness and suddenly having to describe green fields and trees.

I had been writing short stories which, as opposed to my apprenticeship novels, were set in Nottingham. Several concerned the adventures of the same person. One incident was about a young man of twenty-two falling down stairs in a pub when he was blind drunk. I sent it as a story to John Lehmann's *London Magazine*, as well as to others, but no one wanted to publish it, so I put it into a folder until similar pieces joined it. I gave this character the name of Arthur Seaton, modelling him physically on some one I'd boozed around with in my factory days.

The idea of Robert Graves that I write a novel set in Nottingham had no doubt fixed itself in my mind. The accumulating pile of stories and sketches concerning Arthur Seaton showed that he was a young anarchic roughneck who worked hard and earned good money (for those days) in a bicycle factory, and didn't give a damn for anybody. His bones were solid, but some of his flesh was soft enough in places, and got him into all sorts of scrapes, especially with women.

But he wasn't as simple as that, either. Going back to the novel, and reading parts of it again, it is plain that he never was. A simple man doesn't exist. It's just that his complexities may not be apparent to others, and that he is not always able to express them. No whole man is simple, though there are those who have their nerve-ends bitten off with the umbilical cord, subjects of real concern and often scandal. But in general the simple of the earth are only so to those other people who do not know how to understand them, and hardly ever to themselves.

I started this new novel in the autumn of 1956, sitting under an orange tree, and writing with pen and ink into a notebook. The house we lived in was on a terrace above the town of Soller, looking across the valley at the massive 1,500-metre face of Puig Mayor. It was difficult to imagine a greater contrast between what I was writing about with such all-engrossing surety, and the grand landscape before me.

I finished the pen-and-ink work in six months, and labelled it 'The Adventures of Arthur Seaton'. Then I rewrote it into a second draft and typed it to the length of four hundred pages. Changing the title to 'Saturday Night and Sunday Morning', I went to work slaughtering and reshaping sentences, adding and lopping off, and turning each clean page black with corrections, so that the final version, in the following August, was a hundred pages less. The work took about a year, but material incorporated into it had been written during the previous five.

I hadn't read many novels set in the life I was writing about. One of the best was *The Ragged Trousered Philanthropists*, from the far-off days of Edwardian England. Before that there had been *A Child of the Jago*—but it was a very sketchy map I walked over. It included of course that sombre and excellent novel of Walter Greenwood's, *Love on the Dole*, from the thirties. The first half of *Sons and Lovers* was another, though the only working man in it was Walter Morel the coalminer and, being a portrait of Lawrence's own father, it had things loaded too heavily against him by his priggish son Paul who was based closely on Lawrence himself.

Without conjuring up (from the all-seeing trigonometrical point of hindsight) a definite policy which I did not have, I know at least that I wanted to write a novel about a working man who, though not necessarily typical of the zone of life he lived in, belonged to it with so much flesh and blood that nothing could cause him to leave it—not even his mother.

There was nothing heroic about Arthur Seaton, nor was there meant to be. The hero is always in the eye of the beholder, in any case. He was a man basically without a story, and not even typical, no matter what he may seem. Those individuals who work in factories are only members of a 'class' when they band together to come out on strike for better wages and conditions. In normal circumstances they see each other as unique people, otherwise they would not see each other as human beings at all, and a writer who claims to know something about their life would not be able to write with any aspect of truth whatsoever if he did not do the same.

The sort of working men portrayed in England by the cinema, or on radio and television, or in books, were either criminals, servants, or funny people. They were presented in unrealistic terms that working people had perhaps come to accept and expect too readily about themselves, images handed out to them which if shown often enough would, it was hoped, keep them behaving in the same jokey but innocuous fashion. They lacked dignity in fiction because they lacked depth. But it seemed obvious to me that they had as much reason as anyone else to see themselves and their lives portrayed accurately in books.

Writers not born into such a life perpetuated those cliché ideas because it was easier to write to such ready-made formulae, and because they felt it was socially desirable to do so. Those who *were* born into it (what few there were) often did the same because they looked on their past either with scorn or shame, finding, as they climbed the so-called social ladder, that each rung under their feet was made of the solidified mores that despised the sort of life they had come from.

I knew Arthur Seaton to be nothing like the common reflection, but a man who hated and distrusted those who tried to foist on him a personality and sets of values that he did not want. I hoped to get at the real thing as far as I knew it, to produce a work in which no one is trying to 'better' himself.

This of course detracts from the tragic Jude the Obscurity theme, which might have made it of more universal interest had it not been done so often before; but I was not really concerned with that. I wrote the book with few profound thoughts in my head about it, though I was aware, in being amused and absorbed by the narrative myself, that it would be acceptable as a novel.

VIII

The novel went to five publishers before being accepted. It's no use saying I was not discouraged, much more so than with the previous seven duds. One editor wanted me to alter the ending. Another thought this wasn't how the working man's mind should be portrayed. It wasn't how he acted, and a few salient amendments might bring it into line ... I began to wonder whether I wasn't living in a western sort of Moscow. What exactly he wanted I didn't bother to find out. I knew that what I had written was correct from my point of view, and would not change it.

In the spring of 1958 we moved from Majorca to the sea port of Alicante, on the Spanish mainland. We had been giving English lessons in Soller, but it wasn't possible to do so in our new place, so we decided to pack up and go to England. Perhaps we were only waiting for an excuse to get away from Spain for a while.

The flat we'd rented was too noisy, being situated in front of the city tram terminus, and built over a printing works. All in all, Alicante didn't work out. While looking through the mass of material which would have to be packed and taken to England, sorting manuscripts to be burned because we couldn't afford extra luggage fees on the train journey, I found a sheet of paper containing a single handwritten line:

'the loneliness of the long-distance runner.'

Among the scattering of suitcases and trunks, oblivious to everything, I wrote the first half of the story which was to have that line for its title, finishing it in an equal rush a few days later when we got to England.

In London my agent said that the news about *Saturday Night and Sunday Morning* was still discouraging, so perhaps I had better sit down and write another novel. But because she had just sent the book to W. H. Allen, maybe we ought to wait and see if *they* thought anything of it.

A week later I received a letter asking me to go and see them. They did not, of course, commit themselves in any way, but I knew from the tone of the letter that their reaction to my book was favourable. I was staying in Brighton, and went to London by train.

I was thirty years of age by the time that misty April morning came around. I got out at Charing Cross underground station to stroll along the Embankment towards Essex Street because I didn't want to be too early for my appointment. There was a marvellous smokey smell about the bustle of the city, and I remembered Joseph

Grand in Camus' novel *The Plague* saying to Doctor Rieux in the middle of plague-stricken Oran: 'What I really want, Doctor, is this. On the day when the manuscript of my novel reaches the publisher, I want him to stand up—after he's read it through, of course—and say to his staff, "Gentlemen, hats off!" ' It had been a joke between Ruth and me for years.

When I learned an hour later that my novel was to be published, and that I was to be given an advance of a hundred pounds, I went to eat lunch in a Lyons on the Strand, plunged into a nerve-wracking mixture of gloom and optimism, and thinking that the previous ten years had been a very long time indeed. It does not seem so long now, seventeen years after the event.

Getting a novel published at last did not promise any great change. If I was lucky, I thought, I'd collect *two* hundred pounds, and we'd go back to Majorca and continue writing for another year, until a further book came along. It could be like that for ever and ever. But it brought more affluence than that, though not enough to divert me from writing novels, stories and poems—and the occasional essay.

Evacuated

It gave me a sense of great importance when, in the autumn of 1938, I was handed a gas-mask. It seemed at last that to the outside world I actually mattered, that I was important enough to be saved from German gas bombs should they ever begin to drop. Up to then I had mattered only to my parents, brothers and sisters.

And when on September 1st a year later I was sent home with a map of Nottingham showing areas from which all children were to be evacuated I felt more important still. It was a crude map, with a faint red line along the valley of the Leen. Beyond this mark were the suburbs of the city, and if you lived there you were considered fairly safe from bombs. But if your house was on the city side of it, then you became a target, a potential casualty, or, in other words, an object of importance.

I remember feeling this very strongly, as I had also felt strongly the news of the Soviet–German Pact a few weeks before—bewailing it to my friends as being sad and disastrous because Russia and Germany together could pick England up like a pebble and throw it to the middle of the Atlantic, where it would sink from sight for ever.

The sense of excitement at being a potential evacuee (even a label had been given me!) rubbed all that out. My mother and father discussed the pros and cons of evacuation at tea. Already my father had work again, after years on the dole, because of the coming war, and he felt important too, working on air raid shelters with a big construction company that demanded endless overtime which he was quite willing to give.

In some ways they were against allowing four out of their five children to go to Worksop for the duration of the war. After all, it was twenty-seven miles away, and if they stayed behind and were bombed they might never see us again. On the other hand they perhaps sensed (and who could blame them?) a fair period of peace from the ceaseless scrabble of responsibility. They'd been married fourteen years, both only thirty-seven years of age, and though it had been a great struggle, the bad times were easing off and they were able to feed and clothe us in terms which were no longer desperate. And it was just at this point that they were asked to give us up.

There was no positive order for evacuation of the children, and this made it more difficult. They had to decide for themselves. Some of my schoolfriends had parents who positively refused without any discussion to let their children go. 'If we die', they said, 'we all die together.' And that was that. Such children who stayed behind felt safe and contented, and we who went in some way envied them. My parents finally said we must go, simply because if Nottingham were bombed we would be safer out of the way. So I took the signed paper back to school.

It seemed that every corporation bus of the city had been mobilised to take the children out of it. The four of us went up the street to school with a carrier bag each. We'd been given a list of what to take with us, which included pyjamas and underwear—but I for one had none of these things. I had what I stood up in, with an extra shirt in the bag, a copy of *The Count of Monte Cristo*, and the gas-mask box because the string that should have held it around my shoulder had broken.

My mother said goodbye, and walked on her own down the sunny cobbled street back to the house. We were given a pastry and a bar of chocolate each, and guided on to the buses.

Everyone was singing: *There'll Always be an England* and such Gracie Fields hits as we could remember. I was vomiting out of the bus window as the convoy of buses wove its way north through Sherwood Forest, my sister Peggy keeping her arms around me. Brian, who was the youngest at five years of age, normally a terror and tearabout, sat immobile and saying nothing at this sudden unexplained upheaval. Pearl, who was eight, also sat quiet, over-whelmed perhaps by the singing and the engine noise.

Worksop was a colliers' town in North Nottinghamshire, and we went to some hall in the central part of it. There we were allotted to four different houses, and taken by car to our separate billets. Everything seemed to move incredibly fast, because I didn't have time to say goodbye to my brother and sisters in what to me seemed like a real mix-up, but which was no doubt good order to the organisers—whoever they were.

Mrs Cutts of 32 Sandhill Street stood at the door to welcome me. I won't say I took to her, because I was too silent. But I followed her into a spotlessly clean living-room. There was a stew pot simmering on the hob which smelled marvellously though I could not eat much because my appetite was gone. She didn't bother about me not eating her food and was altogether kind and under-standing. I remember the round, rather plump face, and the fact that she wore glasses. She must have been about forty.

Her husband was a hawker, as I labelled him, who pushed a large flat barrow around the streets of Worksop selling fruit and vege-tables. He was a big fat man who drank a lot of beer and had the perfect voice for his job. In the Great War he had been a regimental sergeant-major in the Notts and Derby Regiment, and had spent much of it holed up in the Salonika Campaign. He'd been a regular soldier and, when not pushing his barrow, still walked with the pride and swagger of an RSM. Their sixteen-year-old son was a boy soldier with the army.

Mrs Cutts led me upstairs to a bedroom, told me to undress and get into the double bed. I did so, and fell asleep at once. When I woke up at teatime another boy of my own age stood near me. 'I'm from Lenton,' he said, which is a piece of Nottingham con-tiguous to my own hunting ground of Radford. 'I've been evacuated as well.' His name was Albert, and we were to share the same room and bed.

No discipline was imposed on us. We were free to come and go, except that we had to be in for the cooked dinner at midday. There was porridge and toast for breakfast, and occasionally a treat of bananas or pineapple chunks for tea off Mr Cutts' barrow. His wife also baked pies, and all in all the food was excellent.

It took time to organise school, and so after a time I got bored, and asked Mr Cutts if I could go around with him. He willingly agreed, though would not let me help him push the barrow when I tried, except now and again to heave from behind when he had to get it up the kerb step and into a backyard.

When the yard was too small to take his barrow he'd walk up it with a bucket of potatoes, and here his RSM voice went into every kitchen door, so that the colliers' wives would stroll out to the yard end and do business. I went around all the streets and back-alleys of Worksop, until I knew the town and its environs as well as I knew my native Radford.

At one o'clock every Saturday Mr Cutts would give me three-pence, and sometimes an apple as well. He handed me this as if it were a wage, which says much for his tact. I was too young at the time to be grateful, but was pleased to look upon this as my first job in life, which to Mr Cutts it clearly was not. The smell of bananas on the barrow was very attractive, and once I asked him to sell me some with the threepence just put into my hand. I was hoping he might give me the bananas, and then laugh and hand me the threepence back, but he saw through my slyness, took it, and put it into his pocket.

They were kind people. They must have received some sort of allowance for boarding Albert and myself, but I'm sure it wasn't much. A few days after I'd been there they decided that the patched trousers I'd come up from Nottingham in weren't fit to wear, so Mr Cutts took me to the clothes shop in town and bought me a new pair out of his own pocket.

I was so absorbed in this fresh and agreeable life that it was some weeks before I made contact again with my brother and two sisters. When I did, and went to tea at one of their houses, they all seemed better dressed than when they had been in Nottingham, partly from the help of local people, and partly from money sent up by my mother.

Most of my friends were also boys from Nottingham. We found each other and formed gangs, roamed sand quarries looking for newts and walking the few miles to Shireoaks to cross canals and play in the woods. At the end of the yard in Sandhill Street was a piece of open ground, and on this stood a gypsy caravan of the traditional sort. In it lived a man and wife, a girl of my own age, and her aunt Lydia—whom she called Liddy. They had a crockery stall at the market. I went around with the girl, or spent hours by the caravan talking to her. Once when Mrs Cutts asked me where I spent my time I said I'd been talking to the gypsies—meaning my girl-friend and her aunt Lydia. She looked at me hard and said, 'They aren't gypsies, Alan, they're *travellers*.'

One day Mr Cutts said that a place had been found for me in school. I didn't like the idea of going to school in a strange town, but there seemed nothing I could do about it. I was spruced up one morning and taken there by Mr Cutts. The man who was to be my teacher, he explained, had been his captain in Salonika during the Great War, and they still knew each other very well. This microcosm seemed strange to me, after the bleak non-hierarchical indifference of my Nottingham childhood in which my father had known no one beyond equally destitute friends, and members of my mother's family.

I did well in the school, however, the short time I was there, especially in English. Mr Cutts' captain once gave me fourpence after I'd written an essay (or composition) on a great warehouse fire I'd never seen in the city of Nottingham, a fire that was lovingly and, it seems, convincingly described. I joined the local library and took books into the Cutts' household, which pleased them, because I don't remember seeing any there.

The dark side of my nature came out when I accompanied Albert on expeditions to the market by the town hall. I would stand guard while he lifted a tin of fruit off some stall or barrow. Then in the darkness we would roam off towards Worksop Priory and stab it open skilfully on a railing, going home later with sticky faces and tell-tale eyes. In bed at night I told Albert stories that I made up, or rehashed from books I'd read.

Other evacuees did not like the homes they had been sent to. One boy complained bitterly that he had to have prayers and Bible readings every day, and that if he wanted to break wind during a meal he had to ask permission to go out into the kitchen to do it there.

I went to the cinema more often than in Nottingham. We talked about how ridiculous it was that we weren't able to see a film on the problem of venereal disease called *Damaged Goods*—but on the other hand were able to see such marvellous horror shows as *Dracula* and *Vampire Bat*. The price at the cinema was fourpence ha'penny, and this odd amount amused us very much. There was more to do in Worksop, and more latitude to my life there. It seemed to go on forever.

One morning at breakfast I received a letter from home. It came with no stamps on, and Mrs Cutts said that she had had to pay the postman for it—not at all unkindly, but just by way of telling me. I imagined that my father had lost his job, that he was back on the dole, and that my mother had had no money for stamps. The letter was short, and simply enquired how I was getting on, adding that all was well at home. But this meant nothing. I saw them once more on the edge of destitution, loathing each other and quarrelling bitterly, a complete change of the state in which I had left them, when my father had enough wages to stop them ever going back to the old days of a year ago. So it was with them again, I thought. It wasn't over, after all. I was depressed for days, but I think this was only a way of saying how much I missed home.

The shock of it could not come to me in any other way. The matter of the stampless letter was easily explained. My mother had given it to a girl in our street, with some money to buy stamps and stick them on at the post office. But the girl had bought sweets with the money and dropped the letter plain into the box. Nevertheless the spell of my idyllic stay in Worksop was broken.

I'd been there three months, when my mother wrote to say she was coming to take us home. The Cutts were sad about it, but what could they do? They had made enquiries about getting me into a grammar school, but that would now come to nothing. My parents arrived one Sunday and the Cutts laid out a good tea for them. The war might go on for years, my mother said, but up to now not a single bomb had fallen on Nottingham, and as far as she could see none was every likely to. Mr Cutts was ironic, 'Don't think we've beaten the Germans without a fight. It hasn't even started yet, anywhere. You'd do best to leave them, I'm telling thee.'

In my heart I wanted to remain where I was, but at the same time change seemed more attractive than love, and I agreed to go. If I kicked up a fuss I could have stayed, yet even the girl who lived in a caravan couldn't hold me. It meant returning to familiar Nottingham, but going back or lurching forward was all change to me.

Those three months were a century in duration when I look back, a complete life, an encapsulated stage of existence, of which I've had so many. Or maybe it is my habit to separate all such different experiences and call them other lives, part and parcel of what I think of so far as a very long one.

We said goodbye and went to the bus station. I took back more than I had brought in the way of clothes and goods. The Cutts weren't left absolutely childless, because Albert stayed behind.

Five years later, after I'd started work and bought myself a bicycle, I pedalled to Worksop one Sunday and called at the Cutts. Mrs Cutts opened the door, and for a few moments didn't recognise me. I told her who I was, and then she invited me in. Her husband was asleep on the sofa, and she asked me not to speak too loud, to step by him quietly. A plate of stew was set out, and I ate hungrily after the twenty-seven miles.

I asked whether Albert had stayed long after I'd left. 'Oh no,' she told me. 'He got into trouble, and we had to send him back. He stole.' I sensed the horror that she felt at this, and had the sense to talk about something else. Mr Cutts didn't wake while I was there, and I left in an hour. The 'gypsy' caravan had gone from the nearby waste ground: a pony had towed it to Chesterfield.

I didn't see Worksop again for twenty years. I was on my way back from giving a talk at a teachers' training college in Yorkshire. As I drove through in my car Worksop seemed crowded and narrow. I knew it was no use calling at 32 Sandhill Street and saying hello to Mr and Mrs Cutts. I didn't know whether they'd be there, or even whether the houses would be still standing. I kept on, straight through to Nottingham and the south.

After the above article was printed in a magazine I received a letter from Worksop which said: 'Some time ago, I was reading an old edition of the *Woman's Own Journal*. In it was a feature by you on evacuees, in which you speak on times spent at the home of Mr and Mrs Cutts, then of 32 Sandhill Street, Worksop.

'Mrs Cutts, now Mrs Hall, who is now 72 years old, was informed of the feature and expressed the wish to get in touch with you again. Her present address is . . .'

I wrote to Mrs Cutts, and the following letter came: 'Dear Allen, I was very pleased to receive your letter. Also surprised. I did not know anyone had wrote to you. My friend brought me the journal to read.

'I said it would have been very nice to have seen you again when you passed through Worksop. It seems a long time ago.

'You will see by the address above that Mr Cutts has died. Also that I remarried again and that my second husband is also dead. He died very sudden four years ago this August and I'm living on my own. I am pleased to say my son came home safely from the war. He is married and has one daughter 19 years old. He does not live in Worksop.

'Well dear, I hope your mother and father are well. Also your family if you have married and got any. Including yourself. Hoping you have further success with your writing.

'I am feeling well, considering my age (72). I have had quite a lot of trouble in and out of hospitals. But came through safely. You are welcome to call any time you wish. I shall be pleased to see you again.'

1968–74

National Service (1972)

I didn't think of it as National Service: it was conscription, a fact of life.

Since the age of eleven there'd been a war on, which meant that sooner or later I would have to go and get shot at. Such was the state of morale in working-class Nottingham anyway that most people expected to get bombed and shot at, rather than to shoot at others—the enemy—in any aggressive fashion.

Somehow, call-up seemed to promise a continuation of life in Nottingham. I lived in a house only a hundred yards from a vast factory engaged on full war production, which the Germans constantly attempted to bomb and machine-gun. So in that sense I had already been shot at. Fortunately, being so close to the factory, inside it almost, we were safer than those who lived a mile away where most of the bombs fell.

Going to war was expected of everybody, if you were a teenager, that is. Otherwise you were already there, or stayed behind and enjoyed the general prosperity that it seemed only a war could bring.

My friends and cousins were constantly deserting from the Army, but I viewed their escapades without any moral condemnation whatever. They were, after all, only exercising the same sort of free will as those who went willingly. I was prepared to go, because it was obvious that the German Nazis had to be put down. In other words, you had to die fighting before they walked over you. As for really winning the war, only the Red Army was doing that. The Germans made political realities terrifying simple—which was one of the costs of fighting Nazism.

I decided early on that when I was called up I would go into

the Air Force as a navigator. I'd studied the theory and practice
of map-reading from a young age but, on thumbing through *The
Complete Air Navigator* in the public library, I saw that trigonometry
must also be learned.

Having left school at fourteen, my education would not help me
to attain such a specialised post, and the only way to make up for it
was to join the Air Training Corps as a cadet. I am going into this
matter of early indoctrinal training because as far as I am concerned
the four years I spent at it were also part of my National Service.
One was obliged, in any case, to join some sort of youth or cadet
organisation during the war. Only Britain and the USSR attained
such 'total' mobilisation.

I went along to the local group while still under-age at fourteen,
to enrol with a couple of friends. There I met Mr Pink the adjutant
of the squadron, Flying Officer Pink as he was then, pink indeed in
the face and on the top of his head, a man of fortyish who bullied
us with much humour at the thought perhaps that, though we were
not the most promising of material, we were nevertheless to be
taken seriously.

We stood in a line in the assembly hall of a local school, and when
he asked those who cleaned their teeth to put up their hands, mine
stayed down. The gist of his speech that followed was that there
could be no life for those of the two hundred youths in his
squadron who did not clean their teeth. He spoke as if civilisation
began with the cleaning of teeth. Those who did not do so had
not yet come out of the caves. So there was nothing else to do,
I saw, except buy the necessary implements and start scrubbing
away—night and morning.

The commander of the squadron was Flt/Lt Hales, husband of
the poet Madge Hales. He had been an officer in the Royal Flying
Corps during the Great War. There were meetings and parades
two or three evenings a week, and from the beginning I took my
training seriously because most of it was 'learning'. It was, to a
limited extent, a furtherance of my education, and I saw straight
away that there was much to take in.

Basically it was a matter of mathematics (algebra and trigonometry), elementary navigation (the triangle of velocities), theory of flight (lift, weight, thrust and drag), aero engines (the four stroke or Otto cycle), Morse code and meteorology and so on. I learned to recognise star constellations in the sky at night, and the silhouettes of a few score planes, as well as to write reasonably intelligible English in the various tests.

I went occasionally to aerodromes for a week or a fortnight, sleeping either in huts or under canvas, and clocked up dozens of hours flying time in many sorts of aircraft. Military training began there, firing a three-O-three rifle, elementary tactics, street-fighting. I met boys from all over the country, several of whom were also members of the Young Communist League.

Being a factory worker, and a member of the Transport and General Workers Union, I was left-wing in my views, and interested in the socialist system of the USSR. So I went through the obvious military side of my training in the knowledge that it would be useful indeed when I was called up into the fight against fascism.

After the day's work I looked forward to study at home so as to catch up with those boys from grammar schools who found the tests somewhat easier to pass. My feeling as a cadet was one of slight embarrassment at being in a factory instead of still at school. And in the factory I was occasionally secretive about being a cadet in case any of my mates or acquaintances might imagine I was too 'keen' to get into the services.

Was it really as clear cut as this? It was certainly true that conscription was in the offing, and that the war would go on forever. In any case there is no such thing as the passing of time when you live at the most from week to week.

I reached top rank and passed all possible tests in the ATC, but when it was obvious towards the end of 1944 that the RAF would need no more aircrew, I decided to try and get into the Fleet Air Arm, which still wanted pilots because the war against the Japanese promised to go on even after the Germans were defeated.

I went to Crewe a little after my seventeenth birthday to take intelligence and aptitude tests. The papers were simple IQ questions, and then some naval officer asked me a few easy algebraic conundrums. He also wanted to know if I was interested in sport, and I told him I was very fond of it, that I played cricket and football whenever I got the chance—which was only half true, though I thought it a lie worth telling.

To my surprise I was handed two days' pay as a naval airman and told that I had been accepted to train as a pilot, with the possibility one day of getting a commission—though I would have to wait some months before being called up for the actual training. I certainly felt a different person than the boy who had gone along to the ATC three years before. What's more I had a number: FX643714—which I still remember, as well as the anger of my father when he saw that I had virtually joined up.

The war ended in Europe and in the Pacific, but National Service did not. This was an injustice in fact (a National Injustice instead of National Service) and I would have been more than justified in joining the ranks of the deserters, but for a long time I had geared myself to accepting it. I had trapped myself by latching on to the means of widening my horizon in some way. The extra 'education' I had received made it impossible for me to stay out of National Service. At the same time it confused my innate nature. I had been man enough to go to work at fourteen, but not man enough to fight free of fate when it finally caught up with me. Everything has its price, and at the time I explained it by saying that, not knowing what to do with my life, I 'went in' out of curiosity and inanition—but in fact I was positively willing to go.

The Fleet Air Arm informed me that they would not now be requiring my services as a pilot, so I 'got my papers' to train as a wireless operator in the RAF. Real military life began, three years of barking dogs, of an existence I wasn't used to and would never get used to.

I remember the first day at RAF Padgate—how many do not?—where the issuing of uniforms and kit took place. Going along the line with outstretched arms the various items of equipment were draped over them, and for the first time in my life I acquired vests and pants, sophisticated garments I had never worn before, so that for a moment or two I was puzzled as to how I would get them on—feeling something like a transvestite who finally decides to cross the fateful barrier. That was another important thing for me in my National Service, if I think back on it. First—toothbrush and toothpaste, and then underwear.

It was a rule that one never talked about politics or religion, a clear sign that nothing else was worth discussing. I met IRA supporters and communists, anarchists and rebels and nihilists. I was torn between hatred of the life, of those petulant bullies who tried to make everything unnecessarily difficult and whom we generally regarded as the scum of the earth, and what I found of interest in talking to youths from all over the country, getting to know about their lives, and in many cases puzzling out their accents, and relishing the different slang and dialect words flying around.

One advantage of the first year was that while being trained as a radio operator (during seven months of it) I was also taught to touch type, a skill which helped when I later became a writer. I also liked learning about electricity and how to operate transmitters and receivers, how to send and take down fast Morse on short wave sets that could reach places several thousand miles away. It was something in harmony with that part of my temperament which responds to mechanics and machinery.

The first winter at the radio school in Wiltshire was the awful time of 1946–7, one of the worst seasons on record. During the icy blizzards the school stayed open when others had sensibly closed down and sent the men home. There was no fuel, and we were forced to thieve and loot for our existence, much like the airmen in Arnold Wesker's play *Chips With Everything*. I remember one youth in the hut suddenly bending over his bed and coughing a pint of blood on to the floor. He was sent into hospital with tuberculosis. Everyone was lethargic, grumbling, bad tempered, and hungry. We heard later that the commanding officer of the camp was decorated for his devotion to duty in keeping the place open in impossible conditions. Every medal is earned at somebody's expense.

As an aircraftman-second-class wireless operator/teleprinter operator I went on the troopship *Ranchi* to Malaya. I don't think travelling conditions had altered much since the Crimean War. The ship of ten thousand tons had three and a half thousand people on board. I shared a mess deck with two hundred others, at night sleeping in hammocks in the same space that during the day served as a dining-room.

I found the food quite good, but after a while I gave up sleeping below and cornered a place for myself on deck in the open air where, despite the hard boards, I was comfortable. It took four weeks to reach Singapore, where we disembarked.

There was a library of sorts on the boat, and I got hold of a paperback copy of *The Mutiny on the Elsinore* by Jack London. I had not read any of his work before (and very little of anybody else's, come to that), and disliked this one, so that I haven't been induced to read much by him since. It was full of fascist ideas about the innate superiority of the Nordic race. The other book I read was *A Room with a View* by E. M. Forster, a work which intrigued me, though the style seemed a bit dense compared to what I had up to then been used to.

Life in Malaya was almost pleasant for a while. I flew in an Avro 19 to the RAF staging post at Butterworth, in Province Wellesley. From then on I rarely wore a uniform. My workplace was beyond the far end of the single runway, in a small hut set on a piece of raised land in the middle of a paddy field, and squared in by four tall aerials. By these I communicated to aircraft, receiving coded weather messages, and sending out bearings to help in their navigation. It was interesting work, for I could chat with radio operators in Saigon, Bangkok, Karachi and Ceylon.

At that time members of the RAF were being demobbed by groups, and every month the numbers of the current groups bound for home would be clandestinely tapped into the ether by radio operators straight from Uxbridge where such issues were decided, and passed to all stations in the world by the D/F channels, so that the ordinary airmen knew when they were going to get demobbed even days before the commanding officers of the various aerodromes could tell them.

Consequently when I went to the cookhouse for a late meal after coming off duty the cooks would heap up my plate with the choicest food, while I in return, from the corner of my mouth, would say: '65, 66 and 67' and watch them smile with relief and delight if their exit number was on the list.

Working the direction-finding aerials was a heavy responsibility, for I often had to navigate civilian passenger-carrying aircraft. I would sometimes be 'on watch' as much as fourteen hours, and on one occasion I gave radio bearings on my Marconi machinery to a Lancastrian which had just taken off from Darwin in Australia, and guided it over the stormy Java seas into Singapore. My ears and fingers had the light touch, and if it was technically possible to get a good bearing I was able to do it.

My abilities in this direction were called upon when the so-called State of Emergency was declared in June 1948. A squadron of heavy Lincoln bombers was sent from England to try and hunt out the communist guerrillas in the jungle. This increased my work to a hectic degree, work indeed that now went strongly against my political beliefs.

The bombers roamed around the jungle dropping their loads, and when they asked me for bearings in order to check their positions I was able to maintain my accustomed accuracy, though with lessening enthusiasm. Even as much as half a degree out would cause them to miss their targets (which often could not be seen anyway under the massively thick coating of forest) by many miles.

A clandestine communist transmitter began broadcasting to the people of Malaya, exhorting them to rise against their British imperialist oppressors, and it was decided to locate it by direction finding, and then either bomb it—if it was in too inaccessible an area—or send troops if it were close to some road or trail.

The D/F operator at Singapore, and myself at Butterworth, were given the time and frequency, and told to take cross bearings on it. I tuned in, and got an indistinct reading, but somehow my hand couldn't quite find the middle of the dead ground for a satisfactory QTE. How accurate the Singapore operator was I have no way of knowing, but it wouldn't have made much difference, since mine was way out, which meant another load of bombs wasted on empty forest. There were too many atmospherics that day for taking good bearings—though in spite of my inner thoughts I had done my best.

The war against the communists had little to do with us. We were only waiting to get back to England. I lived from day to day and did not know what my future held. When I set out on the journey back to England I felt fit and happy at the thought of getting free of the Air Force, though still without any fixed idea of what I was going to do. All I knew was that I'd be demobilised with the rest of my group and have a few weeks of idleness before deciding. I lived from minute to minute, the future hidden and wrapped up in each one of them, enjoying the rough monsoon weather of the Bay of Bengal and the Indian Ocean.

In Biscay the sea was so turbulent that many of my mess mates couldn't eat or do their turn at handing out the buckets of stew for meals. I was quite happy to do more than my share. In between times I smoked cheroots and heavy tobacco, and walked on the highest decks to get the best view of the swelling sea. I was lit up because the present was so uncertain, and nothing seemed to matter. I had worked years in a factory and done my turn in the Air Force, and it already seemed as if I'd lived several times over. The only vision I had before me, apart from the stormy and cold sea, was one of freedom, of throwing off a uniform. But it was impossible to see beyond that act.

The slow troop train trundled out of Southampton docks and up through the drizzle of middle England—which smelt sweet enough to me—to the demob centre on the Lancashire coast. A few days later I was told I had tuberculosis, and it was plain from that time on that my life would never be the same again. In any case, it was certainly the end of my National Service.

I was to remember Morse code at telegraphic speed for the rest of my life, and a modicum of military training that might always be useful, but also I had been taught to touch-type—to make with the writing machine at high speed without looking at the letters of the keyboard. This is a minor accomplishment, and not essential since I write with pen and ink, yet in its small way it did help to push me in the direction of writing—to buying my own reconditioned Remington portable typewriter for twenty-six pounds, so that, one might say, there was no holding me back from the age of twenty.

National Service ended when I was discharged from the RAF at the end of 1949, after eighteen months in hospital. As far as I was concerned it had started in 1942 as an ATC cadet. My total time lasted seven years, a period of fatal length that makes or unmakes so many lives.

1972

Maps (1974)

We are all born into the world with a sense of place, simply because a certain part of our senses is rooted forever to the locality in which—as an old-fashioned novelist might put it—we first saw light.

We don't see it straightaway, however—though we can smell it, hear it, and touch it. Little by little it emerges greyly, flattish, without the latitude and longitude of social guidelines; and then as the senses develop and the years grow in us, we see it in profile, contour and full colour.

Our first map of the baby-universe is made up of reality—to a baby. Nothing intervenes between us and experience. It is vital for our survival that experience be gained as quickly as possible, and so every one of our senses and fibres embarks on a voyage of navigation that lasts all our lives.

It is as if, in our unknowing infant brain, we open drawers containing maps, charts and atlases, which we refer to while at the same time responding to all those symbols and realities dancing outside our eyes and bodies.

We are waking up after the nine-month sleep of growth, coming to terms with that gruelling journey down the tunnel and through the flesh-barrier into life. Because our eyes have opened properly, and our hearts are working normally, we are all born navigators, and a born navigator has nothing if not a sense of place, and an anchor-like attachment to the locality he was born in.

So the child has his fleets of digits—ten from his wrists, and ten from his ankles—to shape his first maps of reality, the initial groundwork of all that comes later: geological maps of the earth under his feet, star charts of what we call the sky, and hydrographic ship-guides to the sailor-lanes of the ocean.

His body is the harbour for this fleet, his brain the office of the Admiralty, his innocent brown or blue eyes two lighthouses keeping a sharp watch over his frigates and brigantines, his 'Endeavours' and 'Beagles'.

It is not all plain sailing in these early days. The base from which the ships go out feels itself uneasy in procuring the supplies to keep them going. The very existence of the base itself seems by no means sure. There are darknesses, unpleasant storms, fearful uncertainties, and the sad immeasurable sense of something which has been lost by being born in the first place.

It is this last that finally gives the strength to keep the base going, that allows the survey ships to be sent out, and out again. It is the key to survival, the power behind the going forward, this immeasurable sense of something lost—a familiar though uncharted realm before birth that we can never know again. We thus become dead set on charting the one before us.

There are also disasters to the ships, to those exploring digits mapping the immediate universe of realities. But compared to those problems at the base they are all negligible, all renewable. The eyes of the base guide and instruct, and the different departments of the senses are geared to teach one quickly, and keep one comparatively safe.

But the total and compact spiritual power of the brain takes us out and beyond these humdrum considerations. At the centre of our universe is the City of Reality, but beyond it our first countries are placed, our new frontiers are set, frontiers that tempt one over instead of hemming one in. Soon there is almost as much pull in front as there is push from behind.

On my earliest maps which I scribbled at six years of age on the fly-leafs of old Sunday School prize books belonging to my aunts and uncles (I remember it clearly), were drawn the countries called 'Dreamland' and 'Wonderland', as well as 'Greenland' and 'France'. Out of terra incognita I fashioned my own escape-kingdom, my countries of fantasy, hewn perhaps from ignorance, and of necessity without latitude or longitude, but created nevertheless because my basic troubled spirit felt a need for them. The world was still flat, and all countries movable, none of their shapes or sizes fixed. They existed by name only. The word alone was what decided their picture in my mind, and their minute by minute shape on the map.

We come into a world not knowing what—if any—part of it is ours, and need to put down some survey before very long to establish our stability, even if only to ourselves. Perhaps it can be argued that those who feel this most are those who have been born into a family which not only has no special position, but which also has no belief in any God, no attachment to any religion which would give the new arrival some sort of framework and make his (or her) world self-contained.

Whatever it is, and I don't skate over the reasons lightly, it certainly engenders a firm attachment to the earth itself. If the wall across the street is an important part of the child's map of reality (its scale has a representative fraction of one-to-one) then the abstract words given to the names of foreign countries, which he hears about, have an equal vitality in his brain, and he desires to see a map of this also, albeit on paper and to no (as yet) definite scale.

In the first decade of life both reality and abstract geography acquire their shapes. My own hand-drawn maps of the world were more crude and incomprehensible than ever were those by Strabo or Ptolemy, though not for long, because by the age of ten I could draw a map which was approximately correct and in proportion, showing every country in the world.

I watched with wonder and utter fascination when the teacher in school took a wheeled metal cylinder with a handle to it, rolled it on an inked pad, and then pushed it firmly across a blank page in my exercise book so that a perfect outline of Europe or North America was left gleaming on the page. It was the action of a magic wand, a device made by a wizard.

Opening the pages of my first cheap layer-tinted atlas provided by the school produced a similar glow of comprehension and recognition. The picture was immediately familiar. I drew and copied maps on the remainder of a roll of white wallpaper left over from my father's decoration of the kitchen, wax-crayoning the different colours for the various empires (as they were called then) and different countries.

I realised that geographical maps had much to teach me, not merely the names of every country and its capital city, or the name of every state in the United States of America. (This test I would occasionally tax myself with, and not do too badly over—often it was like counting sheep when I wanted to go to sleep.) Maps not only showed me the names of mountains, lakes and rivers, but also contributed much to my general education, for it was soon apparent, looking at a map of Central and South America, that many of the place names in Spanish and Portuguese had very precise meanings when rendered into English.

It was therefore the first step towards acquiring a pocket dictionary of those languages, and finding out that Buenos Aires meant Good Air, that Valparaiso denoted Vale of Paradise, that Ecuador signified Equator, and Rio de Janeiro suggested that perhaps the town was discovered in the month of January—and so on through dozens of cases. In my rudimentary way, without it being indicated to me, I anticipated the day when I would come across Isaac Taylor's handy little book of the 1860s called *Names and Their Histories*, subtitled rather grandly: Topographical Nomenclature.

Thus began in part my attraction to other languages and, where the maps were of English speaking areas of the world, my fascination with more remote and educated words.

Then of course maps were directly connected to history—in which I had also taken an interest, because whatever one read of history usually needed a map to simplify it.

As a drowning man may clutch at a straw to save his life (more fool he) so it might be said that as a child I latched on to maps in order to pull myself into the more rarified and satisfying air of education and expansion of the spirit. My regard for maps was of course reflected in the tests we were set in various related subjects at school, but not enough for any of the teachers to suspect my secret interest. It made me one of the bright pupils, but not an outstanding one.

A man came to live next door who had been a sergeant in the Grenadier Guards. He had done his twelve years with the colours, and was now on reserve, but liable to be called back should he ever be needed—as indeed he was a year later when the Second World War broke out. Hearing I liked maps he gave me a sheet of the inch-to-a-mile Ordnance Survey, of the Aldershot area in which he had spent some of his army time. Coloured pencil marks crisscrossed it, because on it he had worked out his tactical exercises.

Up to now I had been like the boys who followed the progress of various football teams. My knowledge of geography was purely factual, a matter of memory. The football fans who knew the names of every member of half a dozen teams, and the results of all the matches those teams had fought for the last twenty years, were using to the full the same faculties that enabled me to reel off the names of the then forty-eight states of the USA. There was some difference, of course, because such knowledge is still relevant, but as far as intellectual progress was concerned, it wasn't much.

But here was a map which gave a picture I could relate to the land in my own district. Every copse and cottage was marked, every lane and many footpaths. I could see that with so many contour lines it would not be easy to interpret the lie of the land, but the spot heights and trigonometrical points were of highlighting assistance here.

Most important, perhaps, was the dazzling fact that such a map, with a scale of one inch on paper making a mile on the actual land, could be expressed in what was called a representative fraction, and this meant knowing, if one were to understand the scales of all other maps throughout the world, and bring them into some relationship with the English, that the number of inches in one mile was 63,360.

Thus, by such a back door, one's sense of proportion received a sudden jolt of understanding. Nothing was simple any more. Everything was relative. All sizes varied in relation to each other.

A third and perhaps more subtle eye was opened, and here was a way of measuring it in figures that I could comprehend.

In my grandfather Burton's cottage there were two maps (or shall I say plans?) of the unbelievably large scale of twenty-five inches to the mile—or having a representative fraction of 1:2,500. These cadastral maps showed some of Lord Middleton's estate, of which the cottage was a part. They got into my grandfather's possession because the estate had been up for sale, and he had contemplated trying to buy his cottage rather than go on paying rent for it.

He found them in a cupboard and, knowing my pet obsession, gave them to me, two thin sheets neatly folded, and showing the landscape round about, on which I walked almost daily, in such detail that merely by going a hundred paces or so I had travelled nearly an inch and a half on the map.

If map-reading is the art of visualising reality from the symbols on a sheet of paper, I was here able to confirm this definition.

It is what we do, by the demands of our own perceptions, every day. It is not the easiest thing in the world, but if one begins early enough, then at least it becomes possible to do it now and again, though in certain profound cases only when the sense of intuition is working clearly in our favour.

So I looked at my newly acquired maps, where the above mentioned process first began: the canal was a bending line of blue, the houses were engraved in their true shapes, the railway nearby was represented by the correct number of lines, and Robins' Wood was shown by neatly drawn trees. The picture was complete, as far as maps went, and I could see that it was.

The soil and roads and houses, and even the hedgerows and fences round about, existed not only in my sight but on paper. They had the truth and dignity of being represented in print as a piece of cartography. And if the earth could be settled and pinned down so clearly in such detail, what about all those shifting vagaries of my own mind and character, or the hollows and pimples in the faces of other people? The mind and the body are as different as the map is from the landscape, but we must learn to compare and relate them, just the same.

It must be admitted that, at ten or eleven years of age, such fundamental questions had not been asked, such primeval connections not yet formulated. I was a child who had few thoughts, and no intimations that, looking one day back from the future, and speculating on my early passion for maps and geography, I would ever have them.

But I know that the beginnings of it were there, and between then and that time, a decade later (an eternity then, but a short enough period now), I was to fill it in by spasmodic reading of various escapist fiction, and by pursuing the secrets of maps till the earth itself which they represented seemed to reject me— because there was nothing more that my spirit could take from it— and throw me into the endless task of trying as a writer to map the spiritual turmoil of myself and other people.

Much happened in that ten years.

The war began when I was eleven, and I bought the *Army Manual of Map Reading and Field Sketching*, a War Office publication which seemed at first to answer all my questions on the subject.

One discovered, on opening what seemed a fairly comprehensive text-book, that things were more complicated than one had thought. Simplicity was dead. The utter comfort of ignorance no longer applied, and though at first there were a few moments of panic at the sound of it kicking the bucket, these were quickly followed by a genuine and beneficial thrill which the incipient explorer feels on seeing that, after all, the range of hills he had thought to be the last before reaching his goal were not actually so, and that an infinity of territory was yet to be crossed.

All we can afford to be ignorant about is the furthermost extent of our perceptions, the limits of our ignorance. This thought, a mere gist of it indeed, came to me quite early on, early enough for it to be useful in spurring me to acquire new knowledge and the right proportion of experience to go with it. I was nothing if not careful, and slow, and fascinated—fascinated rather than interested, which meant of course that one learned new things rather slowly.

Fascination is self-centred, and distrusts the intelligence that goes with genuine interest. Fascination is something the artist can trust. It is a poet's sickness that prevents him becoming irretrievably sick.

With a cheap and primitive compass I worried and pursued the mysteries of magnetic variation. Whereas the top of the map had been assumed to be the north I now found that there were three different norths: magnetic north, grid north, and true north—all useful in their different ways, and none complete without the other. Were there then three answers to every question? If complexity is the spice of life, play on. Questions are generally simple, even if they occasionally threaten to turn one into a schizophrenic.

There were three different ways of showing the scale on a map, and at least as many that dealt with the shape and altitude of the land. Conventional signs varied with every country—while within one sheet of the map the convolutions of the actual landscape varied enormously.

And yet, there was logic to it—if you stared hard and let the picture of the land form itself accurately under your eyes. If you were fascinated, you stared, and if you stared long enough, the secret was revealed—usually only leading to more secrets that needed solution. You soon learned to pick out valleys and hilltops, plateaux and spurs, saddles and re-entrants. By the legerdemain of ingenious print and colour, flat paper was able to make three-dimensional shapes.

To survey the world's land-surface with maps at a scale of an inch to a mile (or 1:62,500, as is the custom in the United States) would need something like fifty to sixty thousand sheets which, with all their natural and man-made detail, would provide an endless multiplicity of landscape pictures.

A topographical map became a novel without characters, or with only occasional groups or masses of anonymous people where black dots coagulated into a village or town. One could see why human society had been established there, where the inhabitants had taken refuge in the shelter of valleys and on river banks because these were the easiest means of transport and communication—not to mention the irrigation systems.

I began to see the reason for the existence of the city of Nottingham in which I was born. It was on a river, by which it had access to the sea, and to areas farther inland. Also, there were hills to the north of the river, on one of which—a high sandstone bluff—was built a fortress in the eleventh century. This ugly and repressive edifice controlled movement from east to west along the waterway, and from north to south by the bridge which it overlooked. It was what was called a strategic position.

While this was interesting, it was not of immediate importance to me, except that it made a certain sense of the town's history, just as my grandfather's map of the area around his cottage made the ground that was touched by my actual feet even more familiar.

The area of open land a few miles from Nottingham's city centre, as portrayed on that map, began to change only a few years later, to be covered by houses and new roads spreading from the town. From being countryside it turned into a suburb. The topographical picture stays as only a dream-landscape in my mind. With childhood—the continent that forms the writer in so far as his sense of place has any part in it—it has been obliterated.

There is no sadness in this, no vain regrets. It is so common an occurrence that one is tempted to say it is all for the good. It is another area of inaccessibility, like the scenes that happened before one was born.

The relevance of both are stunning and vital—but gone beyond the dimmest of recall. And if one desires to recollect them with any clarity (in order to explain many things, perhaps, connected with the present) one can only do it by an act of the imagination. Memory is not enough. It needs the lever of imagination to make it real. While memory may make it real to yourself, only imagination can make it live for others.

Maps, however, are of assistance in such cases, both to memory and to imagination. A map or sketch drawn from memory recreates a whole lost world during the reconstruction of it. One puts in a cottage, a coal mine, a bridge, even a well from which the cottages drew their water. On the western skyline you can feel the city's presence. To the east there is terra incognita for a while, until you get your first bicycle, bought from your wages after starting work, and fill in the far-off industrial and mining townships.

The earth is so impressive that you grace it with the decoration of a map. You fix the work of both nature and man in one clear definable grasp. By compass work and pacing I made my own— very rough stuff, but real nonetheless at a time when maps could no longer be bought without permission from the local police because there was a war on. If spies got their hands on them, what destruction they would cause!

I recently found a map in a secondhand bookshop to the scale of 1:100,000 which had been printed in Germany at the beginning of the war—a simple reduction of the English Ordnance Survey inch-to-a-mile. Naturally, the Germans had all the maps they needed, certainly enough either for spies or their army.

All signposts in wartime England had been removed from every crossroads, so if one wandered too far by bicycle a good map was needed. Only those diagrammatic productions of the smallest scale were obtainable, and even then you had to show your identity card to the shopkeeper before he would hand one over. The official guidebook to Nottingham's fair city was only sold to you after the street plan had been torn out by the shop assistant. In a sense this turned everyone into a spy, and me into my own surveyor.

Just as a general needs maps upon which to plan his campaign or fight his battles, so an author requires them for his novels and stories, even if they exist only in memory, or in his imagination. But it is better to get them down in black and white, better still in many colours (given the skill, will and patience) for they can be just as much part of the notes for a novel as those key phrases and paragraphs with which you prepare the ground for one.

Joseph Conrad drew charts of Costaguana for his novel *Nostromo*, and in *Victory* and *Lord Jim* one feels he was using them in these books also, a redrawing perhaps of the Admiralty Charts with which he had been so familiar. It is safe to assume that James Joyce kept a street plan of Dublin close to his desk, on which to work out one or two permutations in *Ulysses*.

Either you have the maps inside your own brain or, to bring to life the imaginative bit of country you see only dimly at first, you draw it clearly on a sheet of paper so that you make no mistakes at least in the geography of your tale. I did this for my novels *The General* and *Travels in Nihilon*, though in these cases it is understandable because both took place in countries which do not exist, and had therefore to be given some form of rudimentary cartography.

For my Nottingham novels and stories, which account for the greater part of my writing, I have always had near me a street plan, as well as a one-inch map of the area to the west and north of the city. These last two items are not essential for my writings about this piece of territory, because I know every nook and cranny, every hole and corner of it, and always will, but still it is good to be correct.

Another function of such maps is that when searching for the surname of a character (and one has to be careful to get one that fits) I pore over the sheet of a one-inch map (not necessarily of the area where the character is supposed to have been born) and choose one from that of a hamlet or farmhouse, stream or hilltop, or some other such noticeable feature. This might appear to match the person to the region he or she lives in, but place-names of England are so homogenous that I tend to mate the names more for the onomatopoeic sound of the thing than to give any geographical clue to the person concerned. Above all, it is important to know what you are doing: to comprehend, to be accurate, clear, and economical—as one would be in actually making a map.

From the age of fourteen my connection with maps took on a more practical form. Because the war was on I became a member of a cadet organisation which provided pre-training facilities for the Royal Air Force. Not unnaturally, I wanted to become a navigator

—rather than, say, a pilot or a gunner. So in my spare time I applied myself to learning the art of air navigation, which included such elementary parts as dead-reckoning, the understanding of maps and charts, meteorology, and radio-telegraphy.

I was already so adept at most of this that within a year I had passed all the tests. Most things fell into place with what I had been taking in by myself, and the additional instruction was now a form of further education, at a time when I would have become totally pre-occupied with my work in the factory and never picked up pen or pencil or book from one year's end to the next.

On training flights I had access to topographical maps, and was able for the first time, at fifteen years of age, to see the land spread out from a thousand feet and to identify every fact and feature on it. This new dimension of visibility allowed me to see the area I'd been born and brought up in—laid on to one grey-green dun-coloured piece of earth.

It made a tremendous impression, almost as if I had grown wings myself, as that twin-engined de Havilland Dominie biplane with eleven cadets in it rumbled across the grass airfield and slowly lifted its plywood and aluminium body into the air. It crossed the River Trent, and gave me my first glimpse of Nottingham from above— a sedate vista, because the plane did not fly at much more than 100 mph.

One saw at once that primitive surveying techniques with the theodolite and Abney Level were out, and that photogrammetry was in—or almost. Things could be viewed from a distance, whole and all-formed, and this bird's eye snapshot appeared to be just as valuable as the dense intricacies that came with lesser visibility on the ground. Indeed it was strikingly obvious that one must have both views, that they must complement each other before the picture completed itself.

When I came to write my first published novel I was reminded of this first flight, because I wrote it a thousand miles from the actual streets in which it took place, and several years distant in time—which I think enabled me to see things all the more clearly.

A sense of place for a writer also involves a sense of distance. He has to look at things under a magnifying glass, and from the sky as well.

In spite of my aptitude for navigation, when I volunteered at seventeen for the Fleet Air Arm I was accepted to train only as a pilot—and then sent home to wait for call-up. In the meantime, the war ended, and even my potential services as a pilot were no longer needed, so I went into the RAF and trained as a wireless operator—for work on the ground.

This too, in my early duties, came to involve a certain element of navigation. In Malaya I was put into a remote hut at the end of an airstrip and, apart from my transmitter and receiving gear, I had some Marconi direction-finding equipment to send bearings to aircraft which used radio-telegraphy to find their positions, in days before radar grids could give it to them with more speed—and certainly more accuracy.

After leaving Malaya I went into hospital in England for eighteen months because I had caught tuberculosis. It is interesting to reflect on this crucial period of my life—the years from twenty to twenty-two—because it was then that I knew I could no nothing else except become a writer. However, it seemed that I had not given up all hope of leading a normal existence because during my enforced incarceration—when I was reading all the interesting books I could find, and writing many poems and stories—I sent for a correspondence course in surveying.

The old obsession came back in my long and wearisome idleness. I studied for many months, and at last really got to grips with the proper science of surveying. In all seriousness, it seemed the only thing I was cut out for, to qualify so that I could bury myself in the mundane occupation of making maps.

I was also at last accepting the task, almost without knowing it, yet with an intensity of which I was not aware, of getting into the map of my own consciousness. Or at least I was able to perceive that such a thing existed. This became so plain and dominant, as my writing took over my whole existence, that I left off the studies in surveying. My mind knew at last what it really wanted to do, and that simply was to write novels, poems and stories.

My interest in maps, navigation, and geography has persisted, and brings many questions to mind. It is certain that every writer has another trade or profession lurking behind his façade, that would have broken through if he had not succeeded in becoming a writer. Many indeed followed a profession for the early part of their lives— or kept it much of the way through.

But why geography, or cartography? What magic is there in it for me? Why did I, as a child, teach myself to read a map at the same time as learning to read a novel? And why did I, as a young man in hospital, make my first conscientious attempt at constructing maps while beginning my first serious efforts to write a novel?

In the beginning was the map, and perhaps I looked upon it so intently in the hope that it would show me where to go, and that it would guide me from the place I was in and didn't want to be in. It indicated to me, in its geographical entity, that there were places to go to from which I would be able to look back on myself and the place I had come from. In those early childhood days I needed a picture of the future, proof that it and I were going to exist, if only in landscape on a flat piece of paper.

Then again, I wanted everything to be neat and tidy—another virtue of the artist, even though it is often regarded as a failure in a man. I needed, in my drawing of maps, to control the landscape that I wanted to inhabit—even to repress the shifting tectonic earthscapes of both past and future. I was constantly trying to shackle my spirit into some blueprint or other. Another name for this may be 'an art form': to bring the dynamic lines of flux on to paper, from which calm state they can be visualised and read by other people as dynamic lines of flux.

Landscape, the earth's skin, we cannot of course control, though the purpose of a good map is that, for a time at any rate, it eliminates uncertainty. I say 'for a time' because earthquake or war or progress can at any moment put paid to that. The western fjords on the south coast of Chile are quite unmappable. But eternity has no place in cartography, either of the earth, or of the heart, or indeed of human life.

Perhaps my passion for making topographical maps springs from my love of the place and its environs where I was born and brought up. And maybe my obsessions with geographical maps comes from my love and concern with the rest of the world. It has always been quite plain to me that the two must go together. I have always felt that real love begins with one's feeling for the earth, and that if you do not have this love then you cannot really begin to love people.

But that statement seems only to be an empty generalisation— the terra incognita of half-baked thought and shallow observation.

Or maybe I was forced into this love of the earth and landscape very early on because—rightly or wrongly, false or true—it seemed to my recently born organism that I did not appear to be getting enough love given to me, that all-embracing succour to which I thought I was somehow entitled. This is no reflection on those who could have given it to me. For someone who was destined to love maps and become a writer, no amount would have been enough.

As a writer, and as a person, one has to take every possibility into account. It is a great honour to be born into the world with all the makings of an engineer or geographer, but a greater mystery immediately becomes apparent if I wonder why I turned into a writer.

When the dychotomy became plain at the time of birth, one felt threatened, and turning to maps was a stabilising factor, giving play both to rigidity and fantasy—that flesh-locked conflict that has to be contained and somehow mapped if one is to survive for a reasonable length of time.

It was a way of fixing the mind, and at the same time recognising no limits to the prison in which it seemed one had been born.

1974

Poor People (1964)

I once knew an American writer in Majorca who, over a bottle of gin and a dish of spiced snails, smoking a two-peseta cigar, would lean back contentedly in his chair after finishing work in the evening, and exclaim: 'Ah! I wonder what the poor are doing tonight?' I didn't try to tell him, because I was poor myself. In any case, he didn't really want to know, because he was joking, and because he also had been poor.

In England there are half a million people out of work, and ten times that number living in real poverty, what I would call below the telly-line, as well as below the bread-line. The gap between the very poor and the normal rich is wider than it has ever been. The adults of these five or six million people form part of those twenty-three per cent who regularly never bother to vote at a general election.

Voting can never make any difference to their plight. It would take too long. They want to get out of it now, this minute, this week at the most. When you live from day to day, how can you believe anyone who says he will alter things in a few years? The years ahead are an empty desert, without landmarks of any kind, beyond the imagination. Poor people live in the present.

The poor lack manoeuvrability. Without money you are born and die in the same place. To travel presents difficulties that are rarely overcome. You are tied at the ankle, and cannot stray beyond a certain distance from the roots of your poverty. The advantage of this is that you become familiar with the environs of your sleeping place, and there may be a chance of living off the land.

Your world becomes small, intense and real. Your senses are sharpened but, strangely enough, this doesn't necessarily mean an

increase in intelligence, or the ability to act. Intelligence is often
stunted in the fight for order and food. A near-cretin, mustering
energy in order to survive, may present a dextrous visage to the
better-off, who imagines he must be cunning to survive at all on
so little.

The very poor are too busy surviving to want to get on. To get
on is something often dinned into them, handed down by the culture
beneath which they exist. They are unable to take advantage of it,
for to reach next week with clothes on your back, food still on the
table, and enough life in your brain to face another week is the
most they can do.

The rich, or normally well-off, cannot imagine how much an
achievement this is in fact. The rich can accuse them of fecklessness,
lack of thrift (qualities that the rich dare not enjoy if they want to
stay where they are), but the greatest virtue of the poor is that they
have learned how to survive without disturbing the rich.

Apart from the natural failings found in people of any class,
they are where they are because of the lack of opportunity to
develop intelligence or learn skill. Their life is maintained by
patience, tenacity, scepticism and pride. This quality of survival is
one that the better-off have forgotten how to use because they do
not need it any more: to keep what they already have demands a
different mental process.

Films on the telly, or at the cinema, giving examples of people
who, one way or another, got on through personal striving, are
enjoyed for the story, but believed only as a fairy tale is. That, they
say, is not for the likes of us. In a way they are right. The poor not
only know their place (maddening as this may seem to many) but
they will go on knowing it until they can get out of it on their own
terms.

The poor live in isolation, unreachable by private benevolence,
goodness of heart, or sound advice. Poverty is a disease, as incurable
as cancer, incurable because the resources of the state are not made
to do a great surgical operation.

How can one define a poor person? When I had some money in

my pocket I was walking down Holland Road and saw a grey-bearded man in absolute rags lying on a piece of wall. Rain was pouring down. I offered him some money, but he waved me angrily away. I should have known better. The poor either earn money, ask for it, or take it. They have a way of keeping their self-respect, in these forms of getting what they need.

There are degrees of being poor. The most common is that of the man who earns twelve pounds a week and has a couple of children. If he is living in London he may pay four pounds a week for a room, and his wife will be unable to go to work because the children can't be left alone. This is not usually regarded as poverty. In such a room you might find a telly or radio. The man will smoke cigarettes, go to the pictures now and again, drink a pint maybe—all in small degree, after his rations are secure, sometimes when they are not.

Orwell did his nut about the diet of the poor, in *The Road to Wigan Pier*. He would do it again if he were still alive. Not for them the simple wholesome stuff. Frozen-this and processed-that, tinned muck, loaves of sliced, wrapped, steambaked pap, margarine and turnip marmalade, tea, flaky pastries made with axle-grease and saccharine, meat like frozen rope—is what keeps people pale and frantic, and just strong enough to work, or strong enough not to. The womb-sweets and womb-custard (as advertised on telly) keep them close to the umbilical cord of the 'deeply satisfying'.

If a family doesn't throw some money away each week on fags and the pictures they may go under quicker than if they do. Their morale cracks, and they end up either in the poor-house or the looney-bin. This is a reason for the so-called fecklessness of the poor: a visit to the pictures is often better than a hot dinner.

A poor family cannot always find a room to live in. They may be terrorised and thrown out by someone wanting vacant possession of a house in an area becoming fashionable. Sometimes my eye catches an ad in a newspaper, of a house for sale, and the tagged-on phrase 'vacant possession if desired' makes me think of two hundred police and bailiffs ejecting a family in St Stephen's Gardens at four-thirty in the morning after a ten-day siege.

A poor person can never be sure, from one week to the next, where he will be living. He has mobility within a wall. To get beyond the wall, into the big wide world, he needs an entrance ticket. That means money, and he knows it. The poor live in a vicious circle, work hard, and pay out so much a week in order to live—an eternal HP so as to get the biggest Bingo prize of all at the end of sixty or seventy years: death in a fine coffin.

There are different kinds of poverty then. First is the never-ending sort, which collapses in death, a poverty in which you were born, and from which you were never able to move. Then there is the poverty of the young man, say, who is to become a writer or painter: poverty from choice. This can be awful and degrading but, whatever he may say, it is a lesser form of evil than poverty. It is a stage to something else. It has compensations.

There is the poverty of the man who has known better days, as they say. This is bad enough, but he knows it is not the only state of living. He knows also that there is a possibility of alteration. At least he has had better days.

The worst poverty of all is that which afflicts the man who is out of work for a long time, through no fault of his own. This is a destitution of the spirit as well as a destitution of material means—the man who wants work yet has to see his children never quite getting enough to eat, who knows that something could be done about his situation but is powerless to do anything on his own. Such a man becomes filled with bitterness—and wry indeed when he later observes his children beginning to acquire by stealth a tithe of those riches to which he had never been entitled.

The poor know of only two classes in society. Their sociology is much simplified. There are *them* and *us*. 'Them' are those who tell you what to do, who drive a car, use a different accent, are buying a house in another district, deal in cheques and not money, pay your wages, collect rent and telly dues, stop for you now and again at pedestrian crossings, can't look you in the eye, read the news on wireless or television, hand you the dole or national assistance money; the shopkeeper, copper, school-teacher, doctor, health visitor, the man wearing the white dog-collar. 'Them' are those who robbed you of your innocence, live on your backs, buy the house from over your head, eat you up, or tread you down. Above all, the poor who are not crushed in spirit hate the climbers, the crawlers, the happy savers, the parsimonious and respectable—like poison.

When there is widespread poverty, people help each other in order to survive, but when poverty is patchy, uneven, and separated in its unevenness, they lose faith in unity. They acquire a sense of guilt, and this is worst of all because it is unnecessary, undeserved, and undermines even further their self-respect.

It creates a good atmosphere though, as far as action from outside is concerned: the government can ignore it. When many other people appear to be OK and getting on then the poor can imagine it is their own fault that they are poor. This accretion of guilt far outweighs the encouragement they are supposed to get from seeing people less poor, whose example they are expected to follow because they somehow have managed to eke out a better form of living.

If a poor person slides his hand on to some counter and pulls down a bar of chocolate he is dragged into court and made to pay a hundred times its value. This is the basis of all justice as he sees it. Is there not, he might ask, enough for everybody if all food were to be shared out? Enough room for us all to live in ? You have to go on working, of course, work until you drop (that's all right, you have to work, expect to) but isn't there an abundance that, if shared out, would be enough for me, for everyone? It takes him a long time to realise that, while there might be enough for the poor, there would not be enough for the rich. Only those who win a football pool see that.

Their folk heroes are those who try, by brains and daring, to get some share of the rich man's loot. He is superior to those who get it on the pools which means the falling in of mere luck. The idolisation of Robin Hood went out centuries ago. If it hadn't, would school books still tell of him? It never quite rings true to them that someone should, as an individual act, rob the rich and give to the poor. That was a way of buying off enough of the poor, who would prevent those not given anything going straight to the source of wealth—that only Robin could get at. Robin had an unofficial monopoly of wealth by being able forcibly to tax the rich. There is a saying in Nottingham: 'Robin Hood? Robbin' bastard, more like.' He ended up becoming one of the king's men.

The poor idolise and idealise those who bring off wage or train robberies and don't get caught. A patriotic Victoria Cross or George Medal has nothing on the thrill of reading about this. They don't expect any of the robbers' loot: the mere act of striking is enough for them.

A man who takes from those who have more than himself is not a robber. The word 'robber' is applied in all its tragic depth only when one poor man robs another poor man. If the first factor of poverty is lack of mobility, the second is powerlessness. There is nothing you can do about it, except endure and survive. If you can't help yourself, then don't expect God to do so. If God helps those who help themselves, then how is it possible for him to be on anybody else's side but the rich? To the poor, God is a Tory, a landlord, a millionaire, a magistrate. If he's a worker he's the sort of bastard who started out with five pounds and made five million. He did it on his mates' backs, and wouldn't give then the skin off his nose.

For the desperate, which means those who feel their poverty most, and deserve it least (if such a thing can be said) there is always the gas oven. But that is your trump card, a fate you often think about in order to get yourself over the worst times.

If it is used it is only as a last desperate defence. It is the great individual act of which you are capable—without asking anybody's permission except that of your own deepest self. You don't sign for it, you do it of your own free will, to spite either someone you know, or the world in general, or because there is nothing else left to do but that—for a thousand reasons. It has a dignity nothing else has been able to give, and few are able to make this last act of dignity. It is the final freedom which no one can take from you, which depends on you alone. It is the ultimate nihilistic gesture which pulverises the hearts of those who love you (if and when they exist), and does nothing to embarrass those who are only indifferent to you.

The poor do not have a common psychology. They are all individuals for whom the rich—who form the state—are responsible. And because the rich can never effectively help the poor (they just don't want to know them) then the only solution is a political system which makes such responsibility not an act of charity but a fundamental principle.

Anarchy (1964)

Destiny of Insignificance

Comments on 'hatred' would, I imagine, reveal as much about the writer as they would inform people about 'hatred' itself. A few thoughts on the subject are, therefore, likely to be of interest to all of us. Hatred is not a branch of knowledge, or a science, or an art, and in order to hint at what it is, I am not going to search out the Oxford dictionary and quote from it. Such a definition, while accurate, would tell us nothing—for in hatred, accuracy is not necessarily a guide to an idea of what it is. If one could get a degree in hatred more people would qualify than is imagined, and the majority would not be adolescents. One draws it in from birth; one is born with it; one acquires it. It is an incomplete, perhaps superfluous vein of the psychic anatomy. The knife cannot cut it out in five minutes; patience and self-respect can perhaps eradicate it in five years, or ten, or fifteen or never.

Hatred sets apart the grown-up person from the adolescent who loathes those whom his elders have authorised to keep him in his place. He distrusts those who say that older, more experienced, more powerful, and richer people know more about life than he does. Visibility from his defensive foxhole is low—he is attacked from all sides—sometimes by phantoms, often by a policeman's fist or boot. So the self-generating warfare is under way, a seemingly perpetual confrontation. When he is mature (whatever that might mean) and old enough to curb or channel his hatred, guerrilla warfare takes over from the open warfare of youth—a strange reversal of classical doctrines. He sees that uncoordinated hatred is wasteful: a Passchendaele of the spirit that may break you in the squalor of borstal or jail. As time goes on it turns to guerrilla warfare.

All people use this weapon to some degree, whether they have been in prison or not. Breaking the law is a game, not necessarily engendered by hatred, or a formulated desire for revenge. The real haters (those who have power) are hardly ever criminals in the accepted sense. A criminal rarely hates, because his hatred has an outlet in crime. An adolescent may despise—but there are many facets to his nature. But the real life-long hater has too much drive and cunning to be a criminal. He has many legal and social channels through which to pursue a career of distinguished public or commercial service, with a medal or knighthood at the end of it. Society's construction is haphazard, infinitely chancy and complicated. The hater can become a politician, may be a prime minister or president engrossed in the gradual bombing-out of an enemy country—in order to feed the respectable underground haters in his own, and give them the satisfaction of knowing that the totality of their anti-life beliefs is being felt by somebody.

When one is supposed to say something about the hatred of the adolescent for society, it is difficult to stop at the adolescent. To begin with, there is no 'hatred' borne by adolescents for society. What is mistaken for hatred (though what may become hatred by the time the 'adolescent' is grown up) is too often the burning zeal of an energetic and intelligent personality which, in starting to throw off the dark ages of environment and childhood, finds no social or educational door through which he can advance.

All that the forces of society are interested in, he finds, is treating him like a colonial or underdeveloped country which is demanding independence. It seeks to keep him quiet, palming him off with promises and sugar-lumps until the energy is dissipated in the first bout of deadening dead-end work, the intelligence subsided into the swamps of sub-literate pop culture, and his senses blunted into the general morass of false responsibility.

Then he can do what he likes. If his character is basically amicable and easy-going, he accepts 'life' as he finds it (he already believes life is 'as you find it' and not what it has been made for you). Or he turns criminal out of rage and frustration. Or he nurses his resentment and becomes a real small-time 'hater'—no danger to society, perhaps, but only to those with whom he comes into contact during everyday life—those unfortunates least able to contain it, who suffer by it, but who are also 'expendable' in this society.

Hatred, in times of war, is channelled against the enemy. In a peaceful and democratic society, where it exists, it is for ever turned in upon itself. Balanced by the forces of love and self-sacrifice, hatred is the great cementer of forces that holds society together. Hatred helps a psychotic to keep a grip on himself. It helps a neurotic not to kill himself. Born out of frustration, a feeling of insufficiency, general impatience with the world, and a blind chronic inability to understand while knowing that one should be able to, hatred is picked up by the young and put to varying uses, either as a means to fight oneself, to fight society, or simply as a means to spiritual survival until a tinge of peace and rationality descends. Often, all three go in equal progress through the head and body at the same time. The head and body grow up, or, rather, become so exhausted that by the age of twenty-five the adolescent can no longer support the deadening weight of his hatred. His imagination cannot sustain it, and unless he has found something interesting to do in life, he simply sinks into the everyday figure of a nonentity.

In an adolescent, hatred is usually a desire, unsupported by intelligence perhaps, and certainly unsupported by opportunity, to fight clear of this destiny of insignificance. It is not an essential part of the adolescent's make up, but society makes it so. It is cheaper to control hatred than to eradicate it, in a profit-and-loss society. In any case, the sort of society we live in needs the adolescent's hatred from time to time. By skilful propaganda it can be turned towards the war-patriotism outlet. Skilful propaganda, and much other work, could also eradicate it entirely, but that is another matter.

Sport and Nationalism

Sometime during February 1969 a certain person wrote to me from Munich—I forget his name, because I destroyed the letter—asking for my views on sport. His request was short, and put in rather general terms, yet my mind immediately understood it in a particular way, as it was meant to do, perhaps. For some reason I copied the body of my reply into my notebook at the time, and this is what I told him:

'I have never practised any kind of sport. It has always seemed to me that sport only serves to enslave the mind and to enslave the body. It is the main "civilising" weapon of the western world ethos, a way of enforcing collective discipline which no self-respecting savage like myself could ever take to. Society was built on "competition", and "sport" is a preliminary to this society and an accompaniment to it. It is a sort of training ground for entering into the war of life. The Olympic torch is a flame of enslavement—run from it as fast as you can, and that in itself will give you plenty of exercise.'

In olden days sport was the king's pastime. Now, it can be everybody's. By sport I mean competitive sport, when one man or woman matches himself or herself against another, either for so-called glory, or for cash gain.

Even as late as the end of the nineteenth century a particularly vicious sport existed in a certain area of south-east England. Its name was 'kickshins'—which is as good a description of it as any. Two men would stand facing, arms on each other's shoulders, and take it in turns to give a kick at each other's shins. Matches were arranged between the kickshin champions of various villages, and the local squires would bet on their favourites.

Just as universal literacy was necessary to get people into the modern age, so mass competitive sport was used as a further cement to enslave them. Like every such distraction offered to the people, the people reached out to it with alacrity.

Why was this?

First of all, sport of big business and big propaganda was allied to nationalism. If England lost a football match against Germany the people were made to feel as if the Battle of the Somme had just been refought (and that maybe it would have been a better result if they'd played cricket). If England won the game of football the Union Jack was in blatant evidence, as a symbol of a national victory. It is no accident that the English say (a false claim in any case), that 'the Battle of Waterloo was won on the playing fields of Eton'.

One might easily think that sport has taken the place of war. Not at all. Sport is a means of keeping the national spirit alive during a time of so-called peace. It prepares the national spirit for the eventuality of war.

The ceremony of the Olympic Games is initiated by shields and flags, artillery salutes and fanfares of trumpets. The honour of each nation is invoked and put at stake immediately the runner sets out with his flaming torch.

It is almost as if sport is diplomacy carried on by other means. Sport is encouraged in schools so that young boys won't masturbate. It is encouraged among the grown-ups, as participants or spectators, to take their minds off urgent social problems, and the need to rebel when they are not resolved quickly enough.

If England wins an international football match, or clears twenty gold-plated tin medals at some games or other, then production goes up in England's factories. Likewise when England lost at football in Mexico in 1970, Mr Harold Wilson, the Labour Party Prime Minister of the day, lost the following general election to his Conservative opponent Mr Edward Heath.

Perhaps Mr Heath is even looking for victories at the present

Olympic Games to increase his chances at the next election! Woe
betide him if England loses against Poland, or Brazil!

You might almost think that England's sporting prowess was
linked to the floating of the pound. One lost goal, and a few more
cents are chipped off it in the world's financial arenas. A few
centimetres off the high jump, and a left wing demonstration gets
too close to the American Embassy in Grosvenor Square.

If England loses, faces are long for a week. Or they might be, if
radio and television had its way, for those media too pander to the
lowest common denominator of nationalism when it comes to
sport. They exult in what is known as victory, but hide as best they
can so-called defeat.

True sport—I'm not sure that there is such a thing—but true
sport, as I see it, is not to set people competing against each other both
in deed and thought, but to work together as a team perhaps, against
some arduous enterprise or obstacle. If a dozen people set out on
foot to cross South America gathering scientific information on
the way—that is good. But if two such groups set out in order to
see who can do it quickest, or who can get to know most—that is
demoralising.

If one man can jump sixteen feet, and another tries to jump
seventeen in order to get a piece of gold with his name stamped on
it—in smaller letters though than the name of his country—and
so that he will become a national hero for a few weeks as well,
that is both ludicrous and sinister.

He is surrounded by flags and partisan spectators while he
performs his act, his national ritual, and all those people are getting
some semi-sexual power-drive from the fact that his jump would
be their jump if only they had trained for it, and hadn't eaten such
big meals during their recent lives.

His power is their power. They see him or her, for a moment, as
them, and them as him. And if at that moment a government
minister or national general came into the stands and ordered them
to jump to their feet, and then to jump sixteen feet the same as

he—or she—they would no doubt all stand up fully confident that they could do it—or something close.

If some mechanism were fitted into every television set which, immediately after the big jump, put out a voice which said to all the watchers: 'Now *YOU* jump—for the good of your country, because those in every other country are doing the same to compete with you, and the honour of your country is at stake'—the nation would jump as one person. The nation in armchairs would become the nation in arms.

The Olympic Games cannot, therefore, be considered as anything other than a mass rally. Under the guise of international friendly competition the same old nationalist values and rivalries are fostered. It is not the thing to engender real friendship between countries, or between the people of these countries.

As soon as a man participates, either in body or spirit, either at the actual place or vicariously through the medium of the television set, or the radio, or the newspapers, he loses his individuality, and becomes part of his nation—with unreasonable yearnings in his heart.

We all know that in the totalitarian state sport is used to drill and make the individual subservient to the totalitarian system. In a so-called democratic state, competitive sport is used for the same ends, in the same way, but so that the participants appear to be competing primarily for themselves and not their country. But as soon as they enter that stadium or arena they are just as much representatives of their country as are those who belong to a totalitarian system. The media sees to that, and so do the people who take up the message of the media.

When that Olympic torch is lit we must see it for what it is. It is a symbol of the oppression of the free human spirit. That flame is a burning torch being carried along the highway, and all sensible people would get out of its way, flee from it and take to the hills. When it gets to the stadium and the crowd roars, you know that that is the place to keep away from.

Gladiatorial combats in Ancient Rome, chariot races in Constantinople, bull-fights in modern Spain, and the Olympic Games in whatever place they are held—it means that the true and human spirit of man is being killed there, the body wrecked and abused, and the heart broken.

Just as all war supposes human weakness, and is directed against that weakness, so all sport is a human way of arranging the survival of the fittest. Thus the arena is a sort of jungle concocted by so-called civilisation, wherein the fittest people are made to be the human measurement of nationalist aspirations.

It is a thing that the truly civilised must instinctively abominate, and then with reason protest against. We must somehow make our sane voices heard—even while the crowd roars.

The voice of civilisation is not measured by the loudness of the roaring. And civilisation itself must not be jeopardised by the contests in the arena. The Olympic torch lights up the hollow eyes of the dictator, and turns all eyes towards the national flag.

After the death of the Israelis the voices of commentators from the Olympic Games in Munich have taken on tones of vile obscenity —real obscenity, the deepest obscenity of the spirit which henceforth will be represented by the Olympic Games.

The resumption of these so-called games in such indecent haste only emphasised their true spirit—that of a host country unwilling to give up its pride, its financial investments; and of athletes who are in the grip of their physical investment at the expense of all human feeling.

That the 'games' should go on after the black-hearted murder of eleven participants shows that true sporting spirit is so dead that one must doubt whether it ever existed. The continuation of the games is a victory for the Arab terrorists, for it is the quickest and most effective way of drawing a curtain on this atrocity.

1972

Government Forms

Whenever a government form drops through my letterbox I want to reach out for a gun. Many other injustices make me feel the same way, but they are a little more abstract and somewhat harder to get at.

But at the sight of a government questionnaire, whether it's for income tax, a television licence, a motoring fee, a car permit or census form, my hand starts feeling around odd corners of my room for the (as yet) non-existent double-barrelled pulverine.

Now I suppose it's impossible to live in this crowded world without forms of some kind. At least that's what people tell me. I don't believe it. If somebody has to collect tax-money for schools or roads or hospitals I'm quite willing to part with my share of the money.

Rather than go through the rage of trying to make out on what lines all those difficult questions are to be answered, I would prefer it if the organisers of these necessary social services pushed a wheelbarrow up to my door and asked me to drop my fair portion of cash into it. Perhaps I'd even chat with them, make jokes and offer cigarettes.

But a form that demands to be filled in or else (a) I get fined or (b) I get sent to prison, is another matter altogether.

My father, whenever such a form came through his door, being unable to read or write, simply smiled benignly and dropped it straight into the fire without even wanting to know what it was about, thereby proving that curiosity was a privilege of those who'd had at least a little education.

He acted thus from a position of strength and confidence for, being penniless, 'they' couldn't very well fine him. And being out of work it would be no hardship going to prison because they would then have to feed him there, and also provide for his family while he was away. Because of his uncompromising attitude no one ever reproached him for 'not cooperating with the authorities'.

Perhaps this was the character-trait of a family whose members were born in times when forms were not nearly so prevalent as they are today. When forms did begin to drop through the letter-box you either burned them or took to the hills. My family burned them and hoped for the best, because the fireplace was warmer than the great outside.

I suppose that as literacy gradually raised its lovely head they began to take a bit more notice of forms, especially when it could mean the benefits of a pension book, or a certain amount of social security, or free spectacles, or an allowance of baby food.

They found that one is occasionally constrained to fill them in because one wants something. If that (as we are told) is the only way to get whatever is going, then out comes the pen and in goes the completed paper.

By and large, however, the feeling of being threatened never left them, and they always approached forms with the suspicion that they were a menace if not handled properly—or appropriately mishandled.

It is only natural that some of these views should have filtered through to me. Why it is so is a mystery when the physical act of writing comes that much better and easier. But even though I can write I dislike being told what to write, and threatened if I don't answer the questions correctly. My natural reaction to this is to stand up against it.

The usual feelings of murder and arson multiplied in April 1971, when someone knocked at my door and handed me a census form, saying they would call back for it the following day. So would I please fill it in and have it ready for them?

I had always understood a census to be a mere counting of heads, and as such I'd have no objection to completing the form.

This one, however, contained up to eighty questions, to be

answered for all four people in the house, totalling something over three hundred answers. I looked upon it as the form to end forms— though I may be wrong. I felt that less intellectual effort would be involved in writing a novel than filling this one in.

My eyes swam when I spread its several large sheets on my desk. It came upon me with sudden and frightening honesty that I could not understand forms at all. Some people are number-blind, others are colour-blind. I am form-blind.

Apart from this congenital malaise I did not see what right any government office had to demand such answers from anyone. The threat of a fifty-pound fine for not filling it in, or for telling lies, was prominently displayed on page one, as is the way with such things.

To summarise the information required would take almost the same amount of paper as was used on the form itself. And so much statistical crap that sociologists love to play around with is boring and useless to anyone with half an imagination. I democratically decided that, since such a mountain of facts might give them softening of the brain, it would be uncivil of me to cooperate. I would act as a responsible citizen for a change.

Some of the questions were sinister. If the form were answered completely it would comprise a heavy dossier on each person. Maybe the government already has such files, I thought, and perhaps not. But if they haven't, I am not going to inaugurate mine voluntarily. Let them spend a fortune on research and technological devices to get it themselves, if they think it so vital to have.

To rob a citizen of his anonymity is to take away his freedom in these days of too much bureaucracy, which is exactly what this census form was trying to do. Such callous statisticians, with the blunderbuss of the law behind them, are the enemy of the novelist, and a threat to everyone else as well.

It was sinister because they wanted to know not only where I was born but where my parents were born. Even if I knew I wouldn't tell them. And even if I told them I'd lie. Not that this is important to me, but it is of crucial significance to other citizens of the so-called United Kingdom who happen to have come over from the so-called Commonwealth in the last decade.

Sooner or later some right-wing government is going to be voted into power by its honourable form-filling democratic subjects which will decide to send all recently arrived immigrants (that is to say: blacks) back home. When they want to know where to send them, all they have to do is dig out the Great Census Interrogation of April 1971.

Not that I would mind being given a free passage to Jamaica or Trinidad, or even Dublin (and I've always wanted to go to Australia) but maybe many others for various reasons would not like to be transported.

The government would get no information out of me for this particular form—short of putting a bag over my head, and blaring 'God Save The Queen' from loudspeakers till I could stand it no longer and was forced to give in.

I handed the form back with the names of the people in the house written on it, the only addition being my own age which I gave as a hundred and one—a not too subtle indication that I wasn't born yesterday.

Three hurt and puzzled officials came knocking at the door in turn to try and bring me to heel. It seemed to me that I had acted in a most civilised fashion, however. I hadn't thrown the form into the fire, which was progress indeed. But I knew that Authority thought otherwise, and that all I had to do now was sit back and wait for 'justice' to take its course.

Four months later a letter from the Registrar General asked me to reconsider my position, and fill the bloody form in or get robbed of fifty quid. Or words to that effect, except that it was written with a kind of sickly politeness more calculated to intimidate than a blatant threat. As I hadn't had an English public school and university education such diplomatic prose was lost on me.

Nevertheless, I was tormented for nearly six months and occasionally robbed of sleep because I hadn't even had the satisfaction of seeing the form go up in flames. Violence of some sort, like justice, hadn't been seen to be done.

Everyone I spoke to said the census form was a threat to their liberty, and hated it. I did not tell them I wasn't going to fill it in. It was up to a person's private conscience to do as he would with it, and I didn't want to influence anybody. Not that I would have been able to, for I think those who made up their minds did so very early on, and staunchly stuck by their decision.

Sixty thousand people turned it down, so I wasn't alone after all. I feel pretty sure that many of those who did fill it in lied hilariously. About a thousand of us were prosecuted.

In court I called the form 'a compulsory interview, an interrogation on paper'. What annoyed the magistrates was the untruth about my age. Such an act was holding the law of the land in contempt. I'll say it was.

I was fined thirty-five pounds, something I could afford to pay, though if I couldn't I would still not have filled in the form.

Unfortunately the census was successful. The form-makers won. No members of parliament had objected to it, nor any organs of liberal democracy. Sixty thousand dissenters out of fifty million was too little, proving to me that the English are a nation of form fillers.

Set a form in front of somebody and he won't tear it up and throw the bits back where they came from. He'll get out his pen and wonder how to fill it in so as to please and satisfy the schoolmaster or nanny in him. He'll let bureaucracy and authority put chains on him as long as it respects his privacy while doing so. A form to fill in lets him know his place, and he loves that. It's probably the same in every country, anyway—with, I understand, the honourable exception of Holland. When the authorities tried to perpetrate the same thing there the freedom-loving Dutch caused it to end in fiasco.

The sociologists have vast rooms of statistics, enough to keep them going for the ten years that will elapse before another census which will, no doubt, have twice as many questions as the one I did not fill in. I suppose they'll want to know how many times a day you go for a crap, or how often you hump a sheep, or how frequently you kick the cat.

And in that time further government forms will fall on to the heads of the form-loving populace. If they snatch out and cut them into ribbons they can make decorative paperchains. If they fill them up with a glazed slavish look of happy acquiescence they will make real chains around themselves impossible to escape from.

The one great revolution left, and the only one that matters, is that aimed against power and authority. Those who use power for its own ends and for its own sake, and never for the good of the people, can only be defeated by an absolute blank refusal to give any information whatsoever.

The Wild Horse

To say that violence is the natural artistic language of our times is too vague to have any meaning. The only 'natural artistic language' is that found in each different individual, who may or may not be in touch with the common ethos of 'our times'—whatever that is. To pin any one force down as a common wave of expression is to set the seeds of artistic death in whoever says it and believes it. It could also ruin any would-be writer young and naïve enough to imagine that there is anything of value in such a statement.

A novel usually treats of or culminates in some form of violent situation. But in order to describe violence, non-violence has to be assumed to be the normal and desired way of solving problems. No novel can begin on a note of sombre violence, and maintain an inflationary atmosphere of cataclysm if any climax is to be effective at the end of the story. Violence is subject to chain reaction, an the chain has to be just as contrived as the ultimate eruption it produces.

A Spanish fiesta usually concludes with a *traca final*—the last lap— a string of fireworks around the public square set from tree-trunk to tree-trunk. The first one is ignited, and sparks off the rest as the fuse travels around the line, gathering speed and explosive intensity, until the last one goes up like a landmine and everyone is satisfied at the outcome of the display. The people go home: so much has led up to even the first feeble, laughable firework. Violence cannot exist by itself. It cannot be the theme of any work of art. It must come by design and cunning to punctuate the novelist's seemingly meandering chain of events.

Violence in fiction does not exist unless you are mesmerised by art into being part of it, in which case you can make your readers or audience feel they are also taking part in it. If this process comes easily, in that no preparatory work is needed, then there is something pathological not only in writer and audience, but also in society. Society is so imperfect that it is often at the mercy of bad art, in which violence is too easy a get-out. A writer should treat violence not only with respect, but also with suspicion, since he is involving himself and others in it. The acceptance or spectacle of too much violence has a deadening effect on anyone, even if only as a barrier against their realisation of what suffering means. To arrange a few public beatings-up on the street (or on the stage, or in a book) is a way of controlling and cowing people's minds, either by numbing their response to it, or by getting them to enjoy it.

An intellectual obsession with violence is a sign of fear. A physical obsession with it is a sign of sexual impotence. Violence reigns in the psyche of the incomplete man like the wild horses of nightmare. It dominates the man who has undergone some form of psychic breakdown almost without him knowing it. Continual violence in a work of fiction, or threat of it, is the mark of a non-writer who is trying to write, a hack who is trying to be an artist.

When this violence rules he is as artistically null as a wild horse. The only man capable of being an artist is he who sees the wild horse, not he who is mastered by it. Man, the artist, must have the power and discipline of separateness. An artist does not work by the crude colours of horror comics, but from the depths of his mind, which like a geologist's sampler, is capable of showing all the neat and subtle gradations of man's consciousness before it breaks into violence.

When the wild horse bashes in your skull during a nightmare, the atmosphere of electric unexampled horror is remembered as a sort of shock-treatment when you wake up. You could never become the wild horse, otherwise this creative element would for ever be missing. The steel-blue half-lit light of nightmare which is the cradle of violence is your own poetic centre. The violence stays beyond your grasp. You might descend in varying ways, but you always come out of it.

But this is only a single spark of your creative secret. If you do not know how to use it, it betrays you to foolishness. If you push it in a false direction, or at a disproportionate speed, it abandons you. You work within the arc of your own light, using the light, but never consuming the battery.

If a writer maintains this harmony there is no problem, because he is then automatically attuned to the increasing or decreasing violence possessing the world he lives in. To exaggerate the tone of outside violence is to falsify even further the stability of his artistic centre. The result to a reader is that of a novel written by an adolescent under the influence of a bad cold. Violence is the pitfall of the romantics, and in most English writers of today you may be sure of finding a good old-fashioned romantic not too far under the skin. The ability to control and tame violence is the first thing a writer must achieve.

If a writer becomes obsessed with violence as a phenomenon outside these terms (if, that is, it begins to dominate him), then he is in danger of losing his power and equilibrium as a writer. Let us imagine him as a man who writes in order to keep the violence in himself quiescent. If he did not write perhaps this violence would explode into crime, and he would be a different person. But if as a writer he uses this reality of his nature too closely and revels in violence, then the reins of art have (if ever he had them very firmly) slipped out of his hands. If he recognises this and is honest with himself then he either stops writing and gets psychoanalysed, or drives his car (accidentally?) into a tree at 100 mph.

Violence without art is an outrage on the senses. It tells nothing, and it teaches nothing. Use of violence brings its own rewards; abuse of it brings artistic death.

1964

Through the Tunnel

As a child, and as a youth, the art form that inspired and impressed me most was the cinema. It had everything: story, pictures, movement, sound, music, and sometimes even colour. It was a harmony of technique that held me for hours fixed in the same seat, the dazzling end-wall blocking a tunnel of darkness on whose floor I sat.

I saw cowboy films, jungle adventures, cops-and-robber battles, Mickey Mouse, and slapstick comics that made me laugh so much I felt I had a knife between my ribs—often like the poor unfortunate in the following picture, who through some slight difference of opinion with a Wild West bully, ends up biting the dust.

There I was, face to face with art from an early age: Indians, Zulus, bandits going down before the guns of righteousness in the land where maxims of right and wrong were carved on every mountain flank or cactus tree. Life was simple, where the gun was law, when I was young and impressionable.

That screen was the dead-end of the road of culture, where one could sit comfortably for a lifetime and show no impatience or dissatisfaction, no desire to break through this chronic roadblock and reach out for something more realistic and relevant. One stayed content with surface dazzle repeating the same formulae of action, reaction, coda and climax.

Other people sat around one in this darkened trickhouse, this blocked tunnel of potted art, of canned technical brilliance turned off on a conveyor belt. After leaving school or factory they came in to forget what lives they led outside. The weight of the world was lifted from their shoulders—and placed on somebody else's, who did not exist. Because the weight was grim, they came to partake of miracles. Some perhaps saw films based on a war in which they had fought, a war whose songs and actions glowed and pulsated before them, and they could silently join in again, and feel good about such memories. Often though, the more distant the subjects from their own lives, the better they liked it.

I use the image of the cinema, but other forms qualify: novels of adventure, books of false fiction, stories of the Wild West, products written with awful simplicity, with cliché prose and stereotyped, easily recognisable characters taken not from life but from other fictions, situations that have been used a thousand times before. Such works appear to come straight from the heart, but they bear a simplicity which hypnotises, imprisons and eventually deadens those who allow themselves to be drawn in, or rush to be so because everyday life is a sack of coal on their shoulders. Looking at cinema, TV, a book maybe, they never leave that tunnel except as zombies to do their daily labour.

Perhaps the authors of these works would call their qualities 'mythic'—if they knew the word, or thought their writings needed such justification. But there is another term for it—'escape art'—the sort that is often a form in favour with writers because, being stereotyped, it is easy to produce and reproduce. This kind of rigid low grade art is, always, 'the art of the Right'—because it is static, either forbidden to move and become interesting or unable to shift into life because its authors connived in this with existing social conditions.

This line of writing is often eminently saleable. It is an art which lulls the people, and the majority of the people are content to be lulled in this way, which makes the writer richly rewarded by the people.

The true outcome of art is different from this. The flickering screen at the end of the tunnel is, after all, only a shimmering piece of cloth that anyone can rip through. The antidote to artistic stale-mate is that writer who conjures up new images, new situations. There are two kinds of writer: he who writes for a public, which means that he can do nothing new, and must use the familiar patterns, or the one who writes for himself and, by mixing in the new with the old, serves the people better. To do the latter takes talent, integrity, and isolation.

A writer is a man who distrusts his imagination. All his writings are attempts to regain the deeper reality of life, to get back into touch with his own inner core and relate it to the social life around him. It is this effort which separates him from other people who are not writers. It is the results of this effort which make him of value to society, because in trying to do it for himself he is also helping other people to do it.

There is always a battle between writers who stick to familiar patterns and those who create new ones, a contest so bitter that it doesn't need other forces to make the task of the writer harder than it is. The writer of conventional mediocrities sees his livelihood and self-confidence threatened by those whose path-finding art shakes the rules and changes them. Yet this is good for art, not bad for it, and what is good for art is beneficial to the people, and what is good for the people can, by a fluke, turn out to be good for the government also. When the people and the government become one and the same thing, the artistic well-being of one will support the other.

All advanced countries deal with this problem differently. It is sharpened by mass learning and quick travel, in an era of dense populations, rapid development, and ideological brittleness.

World ideological conflict (which will take a long time to disappear) causes the fluctuations of the writer's art to be looked on with suspicion. He who writes an unusual book, uses not quite familiar language, lays out an unconventional theme, is mauled by the critics, misunderstood by the public, shunned by timid or less talented writers. If he is praised by some critics and generally popular with the public, then he is succeeding to some extent in helping to do away with the mimings and noise of low grade art. This is good, and even those who may not like it will eventually benefit from a disorder of age-old values which are no use any more in a *truly* advancing society.

The advance guard of art is the life spirit of society. An art which is alive and in conflict with the world around gives psychic energy to those who read it, disrupts and deepens the staid mind. A society stands or falls by the art it produces. A society may try to hamper it, chain it, kill it, yet for the dissemination of its image the best propaganda is art, real art which increases the perceptions of its people, makes them fuller and deeper human beings even though it may at the same time disturb them. Pasternak, Prokofiev, Gorky and Shostakovich have done as much for the Soviet Union as all the socialist achievements so far made—in this respect.

Good and original art being rare, it should be nurtured and helped, not stifled.

In the world today writers are expected more and more to support the societies whose air they breathe and whose bread they eat. This has always been the case, in a milder way, everywhere. No society tolerates those who do not support it. Such writers who do not are rarely popular with the mass of the populace who, conforming themselves, have always liked their writers and artists to conform.

No society, however, can be worthy of the name until it is able to tolerate those artists who do not support it. Most writers produce with no inner conflict what a society requires of them. It is a natural function. But some, the advance guard, the originators or mavericks upon whom the conforming writers are later to feed, should not be called upon to support society in such a way that their art or talent is undermined. Any spiritual sustenance which is to inspire and vivify future art is in their hands. Kill them—by censorship, criticism, official discouragement, lack of publishing facilities—and you destroy the root and flower of your own art. I believe it is possible for the truly great writer to survive all this, but since it is not certain, it is better not to take the risk. A fair balance has to be achieved, in place of domination.

No poet or writer is going to spend time trying to destroy the society he lives in. If it is rotten, his works will reflect it without effort, and it will destroy itself. If it is good, it has no fear of him, and his works may even extol it. A writer does not say: 'I am going to write something which is going to shake this society' just as he shouldn't be called upon to declare: 'I am going to write a novel showing how good this or that particular system is.'

If he is a good writer, he will be saying 'yes' to life, even though the 'yes' may be hidden in complexities or experimentation, or criticism. That conditional 'yes' is more valuable than any coerced propagandistic verbiage. Such a 'yes' can be eternal, valid in the next age as well as this, more satisfying and edifying than that from the shallow man who speaks clichés in a situation presented a thousand times before and which tells us nothing.

In the mass-communications age of today some writers find themselves intellectually committed to the society they live in, but those who cannot make such direct commitment are, by saying 'yes' to life in works of good art, just as truly committed. A new writer, with a fresh spirit in his work, is an asset even if he criticises. He encourages élan and buoyancy, and also helps to dissolve the hard attitudes of mass art. An expanding society needs such writers, no matter how alarming their work may seem.

As a person and a writer I have gone through various stages of artistic appreciation. I was first of all in thrall to the third rate cinema, which presented shallow values of opiumistic adventure. My music was popular songs, and maybe I would whistle them as I worked in the factory.

A drunken man who sings a song which, being remembered from his youth, seems to him the most sublime creation of art, can burn down a house before he gets to the end of it. The song hasn't deepened his consciousness or intelligence so that he thinks twice and does not set fire to the house. Rather, such a song blots out his intelligence, so that he doesn't even know he is burning the house. Such plain emotion, whether it sparks off good or evil, has not advanced a man's consciousness one bit. Song, film or story, it is quickly heard, and soon forgotten. It can only confirm patterns already stamped on the mind. It panders to a mass spirit, perpetuates the barracks instinct, solidifies the herd reaction until it reigns great and solid.

I read shallow novels, saw shallow films, heard shallow tunes in my head. Eventually this did not satisfy me. I distrusted them, began to suspect that this was not all, that something deeper was within reach. So I escaped from the ice-age grip of mass communication products, and began to reach writers (sometimes *avant-garde*, sometimes social-realist, mostly 'classics') that gave more enjoyment and satisfaction. I had not known up to then that there were good artists and bad: the constant flood of the mediocre sapped my powers of discrimination. I had no one to tell me which was good and which was not, but, with accuracy, I was eventually able to decide for myself. When I first read *The Good Soldier Schweik* (never having heard of its fame before) I knew that here was a great book. No one needed to tell me. Neither did anyone need to tell me that Proust was a great writer, or Isaac Babel, or Maxim Gorky.

Having believed that a marching song can be the highest art form, and having later seen that other art forms can supersede it, I feel qualified to write on the subject of mass communications, and the writer's attitude to society. His relationship with it should be a loose one, but unfortunately, in practical terms, in the age of the Cold War, the writer is more and more often expected not only to give his opinion on political or sociological topics, but expected also to incorporate these in his fiction or poetry. Tension can destroy the creative artist. In such a situation it is up to society to protect the artist by placing as few restrictions in his way as possible.

Few writers produce work that is not directly connected to the society they live in. Even fantasy has some symbolic relation to it. It is difficult for me to escape the idea though that fiction or poetry should teach people something since, before writing it myself, I always expected to learn something from such writing. But I didn't want to learn it in a very direct way. I simply hoped to have deep feelings put into me, rather than loud and clear ideas.

The more 'literature' is expected to teach people directly, the less it can inspire. Literature is an exploration in depth; it cannot say to a drunken man: 'Don't burn down the house.' The man has matches and paraffin, and so can burn it down, even though drunk, quicker than a story can be written or told. To stop him is beyond the role of writing—or art. To get him to put down his firemaking equipment and take up bricks and mortar to build a house instead, is also beyond the role of the writer. But writing can be of such quality that it gives those who read it greater dignity, such respect for themselves that the danger of burning down a house (whether the person is inebriated or not) does not arise. At least it may not for his great grandchildren. In this respect, literature can teach, the old as well as the young, the worker as well as the prime minister.

In giving greater dignity to man, it shows people the way to a better life. In this sense, the words 'teach' and 'preach' are irrelevant: a writer does far more than this, if he is a good one.

With so much mass art, the spirit of the barracks breathes over modern civilisation, west, east, or in any direction you like to conjure up out of a compass. We all are graduated, hemmed, floating needles trying to find a set direction, a fixed vector: art can make it more tolerable. Since man has to have a vector in order to survive on this earth, art can keep him on it, in its own way. Good literature from all parts of the world makes for understanding between countries and peoples. This makes war less probable—if the literature, being good, makes for *real* understanding.

Arnold Bennett: the Man from the North

On the day *The Old Wives' Tale* was published, in the autumn of 1908, Arnold Bennett said to his wife: 'This is the most important day of my life! I've done my best. I shall never be able to do anything better.'

He was right. He never did. If *he* didn't know, who would? Bennett wrote over eighty books (an average of two a year during his writing life) but none surpassed *The Old Wives' Tale* in style, complexity and skill. The theme of many of his novels is 'the tragic passing of time', and the effect this has on the human spirit and the human face.

How to show the passing of time is, for a writer, a fundamental skill (not a talent), just as for a painter the basic ability to draw a simple block in perfect perspective is a hurdle to be crossed before his talent can fully flower. This may sound, and indeed may be, old-fashioned. But it was a skill Bennett developed very early because it was highly thought of, and certainly considered necessary, in those days. And Bennett was never a man who wanted to change the novel, but merely to emulate, to exploit, to champion, to push it further into the cul-de-sac made for him by his predecessors. He might improve, enrich, even modernise, but he could not change it in any way. He valued his genius too highly to shatter it in trying to smash the brick wall of tradition. To burst the limits of perception in any way, as far as the novel was concerned, would put his own self-confidence at risk. And he was not enough of a genius to risk that.

Perhaps that was not only because he was quintessentially a man from the north, but that he was also too much a man of his age. He found his profitable corner of the mine and liked it there, for most of the time. With tragic lack of insight he came to believe in his own popularity. He believed those critics who said good of him, and did not disbelieve those who harshly criticised.

And yet, one can't entirely blame him for that. He was good enough finally for it not to matter. Of all his novels *The Old Wives' Tale* is the one that, by hammering away at the same old values, with the exception of some emulation of the French realists, brought him closer to creating a monumental work of genius than in any other book he touched.

Most novels have a chronological time scheme which is subordinated to the cogs and valves of the plot, the flywheels of interaction. In them Time is only another component, but in Bennett's novels it is a deadly hunter who pursues his characters into all sorts of swamps, dreadful situations, and sunny valleys—but which corners them in the end.

It has often been said that Time is his main hero, but this is not so. Every author is the chief hero of his own novels, whether he is in them or not, and Bennett towers above his, guiding his characters from one end of their lives to the other with immense technical control. He gives the impression of working like a blacksmith, using tools and fire to shape events and people on his solid anvil of Time.

Enoch Arnold Bennett was born in 1867 near Hanley, Staffordshire. His father was a solicitor, a 'self-made man' who did not qualify in his profession until his middle thirties, and only then by prolonged study at home. He not unnaturally wanted his son to be a model of himself. There is no one more tyrannical than a self-made man, nor a man more unaware of his tyranny. Bennett had to work in his office after leaving school, in return for nothing more than spending money.

At twenty-one, unknown to his father, he was answering advertisements in a London newspaper. He secured a job there as a lawyers' clerk. Even earlier, he had said to one of his Burslem friends: 'Frank, I'm going to get out of this'—meaning the office, the influence of his domineering father, and the Potteries where he was born and bred. Who could blame him?—even if it had been paradise, which it wasn't, because no place is.

He couldn't get away from it fast enough, left it at the age of twenty-two, and never lived there again. He set off for London one March morning in 1889, already having done some minor journalism for a Staffordshire paper and fallen under the fatal spell of the French romantic novelist Ouida.

This attraction of France and all things French started even earlier. As a schoolboy he had learned a few bits of the language and regarded a good knowledge of it as something that would prove him to be an educated man. Once, as a boy on his way to school, he was told that a Frenchwoman had come to live in Burslem, and seeing her standing by her gate he greeted her in her own language, and received a smiling reply in the same kind, much to the admiration of his schoolmates. So when he said to his friend at twenty-one: 'Frank, I'm going to get out of this,' he meant that London wasn't going to be the terminus of his travels.

Many novelists born in the provinces see their first expedition to London as an important event in their lives—both D. H. Lawrence and Bennett come to mind. A more vital change, of course, would be to go straight to another country—out of England altogether—London being merely a stage in this larger and more direct journey.

Generally, however, they are forced out of their town of factories and small houses by an incompatibility over which they have no control—a lack which they are no doubt glad to have. But the mysterious dychotomy they were born with is merely transferred with them to London, a continuing, half-buried conflict which is the cause of their best and worst work.

The words 'I'm going to get out of this' were not, with Arnold Bennett, a chance-inspired remark that popped up out of nowhere. It had been there before birth perhaps, had certainly been forming all through childhood and adolescence, and came to Bennett's lips as soon as he saw some possibility of making this great break with what is considered to be his roots, but which was really the forcing ground of his art and ambition. Bennett wrote some of the

best regional novels ever to come out of England. *The Old Wives'
Tale* and *Clayhanger* put him on a level with George Eliot of
Middlemarch and *Adam Bede*, and Thomas Hardy of *The Mayor of
Casterbridge*.

Just as London is the clearing house of much money and com-
merce from the north, so it is also for men of artistic feeling, for
writers fresh out of their grim towns—and the sublime pastoral
beauties surrounding them which they often think London knows
nothing about.

Such a process—coming 'down south'—is like being reborn,
like being a baby again, in which one faces the difficulties of a new
and ever-expanding world. In this sense a man from the provinces
is born twice, because a man brought up in the iron-rich isolation
of industrial England, with neither grandiose palaces nor limitless
parks, finds a new, hard, invigorating existence waiting for him
once he comes south.

This, of course, is only the common myth, and it would be
equally hard for a person of the south-east to go and settle somewhere north of the Trent or Tyne. Harder, perhaps, because it
would be going against the continual migrating tide.

But whereas in the north one lives in a town with little more
than a square mile of built-up centre, a homely size in which to
operate, and from whose middle one can reach more or less open
country using one's own two legs, London is so big that the only
manageable unit eventually left is one's room or flat. To reach the
countryside by train or bus takes so long that to make it worth-
while a day has to be devoted to it. And a place where a writer or
poet can't readily get at the open spaces of fields and hills isn't
worth living in. The sight of so much brick and concrete blinds
him, foul air chokes him, and such great quantities of people and
traffic dull his inner senses. It is more human to go abroad—to
France or Spain—after leaving one's northern or Midland town,
than to get buried alive in London.

So, a provincial-born writer comes to London, but often subjects
himself to several years of exile before he can really face it as a place

in which to live and settle down. This exile, in some country on the continent, enables him to get used to the world again after the wrench from home, regain that confidence among his new fellow men which he had once possessed among the acquaintances of his native town.

He never quite accomplishes this, but he does so enough to establish a fairly easy way of living. What he does is lift himself above the raw effects of English class feeling and prejudice against the provinces, and acquires the worldly veneer of the traveller. He not only imbibes the more democratic feelings that exist on the continent, but also experiences perhaps that feeling of superiority which Englishmen of all classes feel when set among people of a different country. This double advantage—while ultimately dubious—enables him to come back and not only meet the English on their own terms, but feel superior to *them* as well.

Bennett regretted that he had never been to a university, that he left school at sixteen and had been forced into his father's office as a clerk, so his periods of exile in France were all the more necessary to him. At the same time he was publishing books, and both developments made him feel on top of the world.

He was tormented by a stutter, and was occasionally mocked by his father because of it. There is no doubt that school must have been difficult also—though he was a robust boy who could hold his own. This stutter lasted all his life. H. G. Wells thought it had some sexual cause from early childhood. This defect alone would impel him to become the outstanding man of his home town, to do one better than those who had mocked him by not only going into the huge world of the south but becoming famous in it as well. In those days there was an enormous psychic distance between London and the Trent.

His first novel, emphasising the importance he attached to his advent upon London, was called *A Man From the North*, and was published in 1898, when he was thirty-one. It was fairly well reviewed, but brought Bennett the total profit of one guinea, with which he purchased a new hat.

Joseph Conrad wrote to him, 'A Man From the North has inspired me with the greatest respect for your artistic conscience. I am profoundly impressed with the achievement of style. The root of the matter—which is expression—is there, and the sacred fire, too. I hope you will give me the credit for understanding what you have tried for there. My dear sir, I do envy you the power of coming so near to your desire.'

Who would not give one's right arm for such praise from Conrad, one of the greatest masters of English prose? (It is ironic, but gratifying to me, that England's best novelist was a Pole.)

By this time Bennett had left the lawyers' office, and earned his living by journalism and editorial work, and also by teaching journalism, as well as by other writings. He lived in Chelsea. In the autumn he paid his first visit to Paris. It did not come up to his expectations, though the effect on him was rather like that of an underwater delayed action mine which was only to explode on subsequent visits. All this first trip did was to make him realise that, in spite of his sojourn in Chelsea, he was still very much the unlettered, unsophisticated man from the north. He was so unsophisticated perhaps that he did not have enough courage to stay on in Paris.

But six years later he was back there. In the meantime his father had died. He had published Anna of the Five Towns. He was thirty-six years of age, and felt that he was now approaching the height of his powers as a novelist.

Eating in his usual restaurant one evening, he sat opposite a rather bizarre fat woman beholden to many parcels, wearing a cloak and a 'light-puce flannel dress'. She was one of those eccentric people who live alone, sensitive, touchy, and not the sort of person (Bennett observed) that you want to look at while eating your dinner. From this sight of her he thought of writing a story called 'The History of Two Old Women'. He would give this woman a sister, as fat as herself, and recount how one had been rather ordinarily married, and had become a widow. The other would have been a whore. In old age they would live together again. One of the waitresses in the restaurant was a beautiful pale young girl, and he saw that this fat disagreeable woman—who had meanwhile found herself a new place, being affected by his unspoken dislike—might once have been as pleasant and beautiful as she.

He began *The Old Wives' Tale* five years later, on October 8th 1907, at Fontainebleau where, with his wife, he had rented a house at thirty-six pounds a year. In the years from 1906–9 his earnings averaged eleven pounds a week, this only after the most prodigious amount of work.

The average labourer in England was lucky to knock up one pound a week, and a clerk might take home two or three. Even so, Bennett must sometimes have regretted giving up more secure commissions in London, and taking to the uncertain and less lucrative life of a freelance abroad.

For many years, even before the germ of *The Old Wives' Tale* manoeuvred and insinuated itself into his brain in the Paris restaurant, he had been contemplating an English equivalent of Maupassant's *Une Vie*—the story of a woman's life. Yet lest he be accused of imitating Maupassant, he decided to make his book the story of *two* women, who were sisters.

The novel begins in the 1850s, in a draper's shop overlooking the market square of Bursley—one of his Five Towns. Events in the first part of the book take place at least twenty years before Bennett's birth—which makes it to some extent historical. In this way he dealt with the solid feel of nineteenth-century commercial England in all its parsimonious brutality and strange flavour of romance.

The two sisters spend their youth together. Sophia is beautiful and clever. When I say she is unpredictable I mean that she is far from being a simple person. Constance is obedient, quiet, moulded temperamentally by the traditions and wishes of her parents. Possibly between them they form the two basic sides of Arnold Bennett's own character which tried to fight themselves out on the battleground of his novels. Their lives diverge. Sophia's takes her to France and thirty-odd years in Paris, with a husband who soon abandons her to the hardship of earning her own living in a strange country. The Franco–Prussian war is about to open, and the uncertainties of the siege and the Commune to overwhelm Paris.

In the meantime Constance is leading an ordinary existence with her husband, who has taken over the family shop in Bursley, and a child. It is a humdrum life vividly heightened by Bennett's skill, and love of subject. The pages set in Bursley have more life and poetry, even though those placed in France of the seventies cover more exciting and dangerous events.

Wherever Bennett went, and in whatever he wrote, he carried a fond regard for the Potteries. It is on record that during his life away from the Five Towns he could never resist—when out at dinner—lifting the plates to look at the Potteries trade mark.

Sophia and Constance come back together again when they are both about sixty years of age. It seems strange that Bennett considers this to be old, treating the sisters at this time as if they are practically senile. He himself died at the comparatively young old age of sixty-four—and possibly considered old age to be the age you die at, no matter how many years are in the bucket.

The reader though, right from the youth of Sophia and Constance, sees them actually changing and growing old with a slow-moving subtlety that is astonishing in its technique. In flesh-and-blood their faces give away to time, their circumstances alter, and their ideas become more fixed, more divergent from each other. It seems they have grown apart forever, but Bennett shows, when they meet again, that the unique human spirit in each of them is less rigid than had been thought. At a certain cost to the individuality it can be bent, brought towards a meeting point. When this price, of two elderly disparate people who wish to live together, has been paid, both cease to be the distinctive personalities they were when younger and living apart. This may be why some critics complain that the last part of *The Old Wives' Tale* is not so moving as those which precede it. Yet the diminution of excitement is more moving than all the rest simply because it is more human, truthful and tragic. These are the hallmarks of childhood and old age.

Bennett, though not a poet, used concise and poetic imagery. Regarding telegraph wires: 'One could imagine the messages concerning prices, sudden death, and horses, in their flight through the wires under the feet of birds.' The order of contents in these messages is interesting when one thinks not only of the priorities in Bennett's life, but also those in his work. People are moved by certain values. First come prices and money; then death (time); and finally horses and birds, meaning animal energy and unattainable freedom.

Sophia's first reactions to love as a young girl: 'She was drunk; thoughts were tumbling about in her brain like cargo loose in a rolling ship.' Later, on the death of her father, and the strong ideals that went with him into the grave, Bennett observes: 'It is thus that ideals die; not in the conventional pageantry of honoured death, but sorrily, ignobly, while one's head is turned—'

Thus speaks the realist who, in these socially exact novels of the English lower middle class allows no trace of idealism (or radical politics) to enter—certainly not to prosper. A French Empire collapses around one of his heroines, the French Commune grows and is smashed unmercifully to the ground, but all she thinks of is hoarding food and charging her boarding house guests as much as she can get away with. A true daughter of Victorian England!

Constance wonders what was the purpose of her sister's life. Bennett covers more than half a century in the lives of a group of Midlands people, and at the end of the book he can only ask himself what has been the point of their existence. To live, one might have told him, in order that life will be better for those that come after us. But for the novelist this is not enough. It is no answer.

Bennett states the tragedy, tells the story, and does not search for answers—except perhaps those unimportant ones unfolded in his tale, that pose no questions. Constance should have wondered what the purpose of her own—as yet unended—life will have been. But she cannot, because Bennett's own was far from finished.

Bennett was one of the few English novelists to portray ordinary people in realistic terms and not as caricatures. Constance, Samuel Povey the draper's assistant, Maggie the servant, Gerald Scales, Sophia, Mrs Baines—none have that flimsy and whimsy combination that tends to amuse and obscure rather than properly open the blinds. He puts everyone in their place with such social exactness that one often gets the impression he is revelling in the highly compartmented life of late Victorian England. He talks, for instance, of the outrages of the workers during the Reform Riot of 1832—a mass uprising of people who, after all, wanted only a rough form of human rights.

His attitude to federation of the Five Towns into 'England's twelfth largest city' is equally ironic and disapproving. But this book, after all, is an 'old wives' tale', one which tries to show that stay-at-homes come out better in the end than erring daughters (or sons) who light off for foreign places. Maybe there was something then in this maxim for Bennett himself.

He was a man who was never sure whether or not he'd done right—except in his novels, which not only earned him money but which were his only reasons for being alive. His wisdom in knowing this, and pursuing it with great energy to the end, made him truly wise, if not really great.

Towards the end of her life, Constance has a moment of doubt as to the efficacy—and the necessity—of English puritan values, which suggests she might not have been sure that her sister's adventurous (and more tragic) life was so empty after all. Other lives, too often for our own good, seem to be more exciting than the ones we scratch along with in our humdrum ways. But Sophia and Constance, by agreeing to live together in their old age, finally recognise stalemate in this respect.

The Old Wives' Tale sold hardly any copies in the first month. Then, probably because of an enthusiastic review by H. G. Wells, it went into a modest second edition, and began to sell steadily. It became successful in America and, due to the gathering momentum of its sales there, was pulled out of its slough in England. But it never became one of the renowned best sellers during Bennett's lifetime. Perhaps this was because in many respects it was too much like other novels of the day, and that it needed more time to show what really unique qualities it had—to show that it stood, as it were, head and shoulders above the rest.

Clayhanger, which followed in 1910, has the stature of *The Old Wives' Tale*, but is a more poetic novel in that the final great pages of it are dominated by Hilda Lessways, who is Bennett's most tantalising female character. After the initial praise of *The Old Wives' Tale* he was anxious lest the reviewers do a hatchet job on *Clayhanger*—compare it disadvantageously to the former in lieu of finding much else to say. John Galsworthy in fact wrote to say that he preferred *The Old Wives' Tale*.

Bennett's works were basically extrovert. He never reached—or searched for—the golden chaos that lies beneath the surface of a person (behind their eyes, as it were) and tried to make some sort of order out of it. The order was already there, and all he did was elaborate on it, show the misfortune or folly of people who couldn't help but deviate from it.

He influenced many other writers—whether they knew it or not, acknowledged it or not. D. H. Lawrence's first novel *The White Peacock* was published three years after *The Old Wives' Tale*, and nine years after *Anna of the Five Towns*. Cyril, the insipid hero of *The White Peacock*, has much the same aura about him as Constance's son Cyril in *The Old Wives' Tale*.

Lawrence admitted that he wanted to write a novel that would do for Eastwood, Nottinghamshire, what Bennett had done for the Potteries. The result was *The Lost Girl*—or the first half of it. There is also something similar in the middle of this book to a central section of *The Old Wives' Tale*. Bennett gives all French conversations in an English which is a stilted direct translation, creating an (unintentional) comic effect. And in *The Lost Girl* Lawrence gets his main character, Alvina Houghton, involved in the equal linguistic folly of the circus group of the Natcha-Kee-Tawaras. Lawrence had no great respect for Bennett, but the influence in his early works is unmistakable.

The few similarities between the two men only point out how fundamentally different they were—both in writing and in temperament. Lawrence did not stay in London. He took himself to other countries, where he could look with scorn on the sort of values Bennett (as a more typical man from the north) worshipped. He could mock at them from a safe distance, and get on with his more purely creative work, poorer perhaps, but more dedicated.

Bennett, however, was yet to produce another fine book, *Riceyman Steps*. Wells wrote to him '. . . I have to join the chorus. *Riceyman Steps* is a great book. I hate to go back on an old friend, but I think it as good as or better than *The Old Wives' Tale*.' Conrad was 'wholly delighted' with it. Thomas Hardy 'was absolutely absorbed by it'.

This novel about a miserly bookseller, and his servant girl Elsie, is a book that has probably never been matched in English for its perfect harmony between style and story. It runs on castors, as they say, yet because of its subject leaves one with the feeling of having read something profound and satisfying.

Bennett did a huge amount of journalism during his lifetime. He was obsessed with the number of words he could turn out in a year—so many hundred thousand during the twelve-month, so many thousand words a day. In 1908 he was pleased to note that his output had totalled '423,500 words'—which almost makes him a Stakhanovite of English letters.

This was a time when his earnings averaged eleven pounds a week. As always, literary reputation was far higher than the reward. He was also pleased to note during the twenties, however, that his work was being paid for at the rate of half-a-crown a word—and he was irked that he wasn't getting as much as Kipling or Eden Philpotts.

He had a country house and a yacht, and the man from the north was now living the life of a rich man of the time—in the south. Yet when he died—of typhoid fever—there were unfounded rumours that he hadn't left enough money to pay the milk bill. During his final illness the sympathetic Borough Council permitted straw to be laid along Marylebone Road outside, to deaden traffic noise.

In matters of style Bennett could not be compared with the more *avant-garde* writers about to burst on the literary scene in the twenties. Yet if he was at the ending of a great stream of English writing, he was also in at the beginning of that more modern literature that has kept its scenery in industrial England. There have been many novelists from the north after him, and the many who are writing now have practically taken over the mainstream of English writing.

If Bennett as a novelist was an 'opencast miner', modern writers of the north seem to prefer labouring more underground. Since Bennett's day writers have moved away from novels which have breadth and scale. Time is not the slave-driver it once was—though who is to say they are not poorer for it? Pace changes, values alter, wars come and go—here today and into the middle of next week tomorrow, dragging with us the snapped shackles of undigested years that will gnaw us later on. For everything has its price. Everything exacts its toll.

Modern writers often achieve effect by using a style based on common rhythms and usages of speech, whereas Bennett's language was in the straightforward, exterior, rhetorical manner of the late nineteenth century. Real English, some would maintain.

Why does it sometimes seem as if the north is crowding out the south in the world of English letters? Is the north more 'romantic' than the south in that it produces more exciting literary figures and works? Is it because life is harder in the north, landscape more spectacular, people less open and expressive, though at the same time more friendly? Is it because the north is grimmer, and the few words spoken there are more vivid, so that when a young man finds the dam of his self-expression broken the fresh words tumble out and form their own unique rivers? I have never believed that, being from the Midlands.

They are the questions of a southerner. Maybe they are asked because a man from the north isn't expected to be a writer at all, is still looked on as a rarity, a freak, so that when he does appear (bog mud and iron-filings clinging to his boots) he is noticed more than twenty writers from the south.

When I was seventeen I came to London for the first time, on a day return. It was VJ Day, and everyone was in the streets cheering, rushing about in a frenzied way. I was with a friend, and it was easy to get about because the transport men on the underground didn't seem interested in taking people's tickets. Travel was free for all, so we went everywhere by tube, from one part of London to another, from one central station to the next. We would get out where the impulse moved us, surfacing to the pungent strange air and milling with the celebrating mob, then popping underground again to come up somewhere else a few minutes later. It was as if we had to draw sustenance from the marvellous machine of the running underground railway. It seemed an unreal town, and because I didn't see engineering works lining the Mall, and factories along Oxford Street, and back-to-backs on Hyde Park, I was rather contemptuous of it, and assumed that London didn't have any factories at all. I had no desire to live there, for the next seventeen years at any rate. Next day I was back again in my factory, saying what a wonderful place London was. All the same it was real enough. Hadn't we seen it on the pictures, and heard it on the wireless? How was it that the reality and the dream never seemed the same?

Basically, people from the north seem more fatally impregnated with their landscape than people who live in the south. It's not that they love it more, but because it's harsher (and it is) they have more affection for the factory chimneys, the coombs and crags, the Severn at Ironbridge seen from afar like a silvery anaconda smashed to death among wooded Shropshire hills, the vast secret manufactories among black valleys, diseased kilns, disused gin-pits and sucked out canals with their rotting lock-gates, forges and foundries, tips and slag heaps and smelting works, churned earth making the aftermath of the Somme battles look like landscape for a Surrey cricket match—these scenes (and life among them) form the picture of a writer's subconscious. Poets and writers can never forget or forgive a hard landscape, mistress or mother.

When a man beats a retreat from such items littering the soul he has to pay them homage for the rest of his life for letting him go, but a tax must also be handed over to that part of the southern world which has accepted him. Thrust out of his own environment either by a socially-impaired character or by a poetic lust to see the whole earth and not only his birthplace, he has to make a go of it in order to survive spiritually in so strange a place as London and the south. Its so-called softness is destructive, and has to be fought by a mad kind of industry, the only thing of value perhaps that he brought with him.

So Bennett had his thousand words a day, his eighty books that saved him from collapse till he was sixty-four. Even then he only died because, foolishly going against the advice of the waiter, he drank unboiled water in a Paris restaurant. 'If all the French people in Paris drink it,' he scoffed, 'what have I to fear?'

It is easy to imagine what exiled Sophia of *The Old Wives' Tale* would have said to that: 'In the Five Towns you can drink tap water, of course. But in Paris? You should know better.' Like Sophia then, he paid for the youthful desertion of his birthplace which, indeed, had as strong a pull on him as Darius Clayhanger had on his sensitive son Edwin.

Bennett, together with those other fashionable literary giants— Wells, Shaw, Galsworthy—who became legends at the apex of their working lives, suffered from his fame. Public recognition may hone off the trajectory of an artist's hitherto hidden rise, and he then has to fight for his creative spirit like a drowning man latches on to the straw that might save him.

When a man's personality is set above his work no contemporary criticism is to be relied on—if, that is, *any* contemporary criticism can ever be relied upon or trusted. A reviewer writes only for himself, as any self-respecting writer also does, and the two shall never meet. A writer's own estimate of himself may become perilously inaccurate in these rough seas. Bennett should have given us more good novels than *The Old Wives' Tale, Clayhanger,* or *Riceyman Steps.* One great novel may be enough from a writer, yet ten or twenty good ones are not enough.

Writers are both victims and heroes of fate. I suppose that has been said before, but there's never any harm in saying it again— above all about Arnold Bennett.

'Che' Guevara

In the autumn of 1968 I was asked by Tony Richardson to write a film script about the life of Ernesto 'Che' Guevara, the Argentinian doctor who became a marxist-revolutionary and took a leading part in the Cuban war of independence against the dictator Fulgencio Batista. This guerrilla struggle ended in January 1959, and after some years holding various ministerial posts in the new Cuban government, Guevara again took part in armed revolutionary activity which ended in his death.

I had made it a rule never to do a film script other than from one of my own stories or novels, but 'Che' Guevara was a man whose career and personality interested me, and I had always read his works with great attention. So in an excess of self-confidence—though after some discussion—I accepted the task. Being absorbed, and even at times obsessed, by his writing as a revolutionary fighter and tactician, I wanted also to find out what he was like as a person, to discover that area of him as a man which would bring the two facets together.

The work was difficult, and lasted nearly a year. I read and re-read Guevara's own books on the Cuban Revolutionary War, and his volume on Guerrilla Warfare, as well as his diary of the Bolivian struggle—essential documents towards the comprehension of his thought and aims.

Guevara, with a volatile and impatient spirit, had seen too much wretchedness in South America not to be moved into action by it. He was a frail man, in spite of photographs which might suggest otherwise, and suffered frequently from attacks of asthma, which must have presented him on each occasion with the tangible threat of death. Asthma is a physical manifestation of extreme terror, of darkness and final oblivion. As a child his mother was always trying to force him back into the darkness of too much care, and the enclosing warmth of more clothes than he needed to wear. Maybe his asthmatic attacks were, at first, his reaction against this, and later of profound despair and irritability at the constricting world of that Argentinian middle-class life into which he was born—and perhaps indeed of life itself. In the Middle Ages, according to Robert Burton, asthma was put down to hypochondriacal melancholy.

However it was, in order to surmount it, Guevara developed certain great and simple ideas. The qualities which enabled him to do so made him immortal in the hearts of certain oppressed people. They also made him vulnerable, and led him to an early death. To those who killed him he was an outlaw, and a dangerous one. When he carried his ideas of insurrection to Bolivia an army was set on him, and his imperfect choice of that country made his downfall certain.

The book called *Ernesto* written by his first wife Hilda Gadea, ends with his going to Cuba with Fidel Castro's band to begin the war against Batista—that is to say, quite early on in his career. The Cuban campaign was successful, whereas the later Bolivian struggle was not. It might be of interest to note why this was so, though at the same time admitting that it is perhaps too easy to look back, and give reasons why one thinks a person made certain mistakes. It is a different matter at the time they were being made, when one could only hope instead of criticise. Certainly Guevara must have carefully considered the problems and situation of Bolivia before deciding to make that country the centre of his later revolutionary operations.

The prime advantage was its proximity to four other South American republics—Brazil, Paraguay, Argentina and Chile, and with lines of communication running up to Peru. He reasoned that if he could create revolution in one, then there would be a good chance that the others would follow—or be pulled in.

A second point in favour of Bolivia was its strong communist party, an advantage however that did not live up to its promise.

Many communists in that country considered that the time was not ripe for the sort of insurrection Guevara had in mind—and in any case they would have preferred it to be led by a native-born Bolivian instead of someone from the Argentine.

A third reason was, for Guevara, that Bolivia had a good and recent record of insurrection, and that the ever-militant tin-miners might be induced to come out once more into the open if he and his 'foco' could initiate the fire-fight.

However, there were fatal disadvantages. The area chosen was sparsely inhabited, and many of the people did not even speak Spanish. The terrain was simply too difficult, the more so because there was not a large sympathetic population to draw on. Also the area was too far from the tin-miners of the Andes from among whom, with more proximity and persuasion, Guevara might have gained a certain number of courageous and vital recruits for his cause.

The main mistake, however, was that he turned the classic theory of revolutionary warfare on its head. The first stage should have been to initiate a fundamental propaganda campaign, possibly lasting some years, to persuade and educate the people and bring them over to his side. This would be followed then, and only then, by sporadic guerrilla ambushes, always striking when the enemy is at a disadvantage, and slowly bleeding his armed forces to death while at the same time increasing the power of the revolutionary side. This stage might also last for some time. But if successful it would emerge into open warfare and eventually complete the defeat of the government forces.

Guevara, however, sought to *begin* with open warfare in order to persuade an apathetic population that violence was the only way to change their miserable conditions, and that the power that was oppressing them was not invulnerable to attack. He may have been right in that there was no other way to do it. But it was this, coupled with other adverse factors, which foredoomed his venture from the start.

The first quality a revolutionary leader must have is that of patience. He should be able to work with nature, and most of the time with the speed of nature—which is extremely slow. The revolutionary time-scheme is often one of evolution, egged on by occasional lightning strokes.

This gift of patience, which Guevara had in some measure during his first campaign in Cuba, did not return to him in Bolivia, possibly because, looking back on the Cuban revolution, he saw it as having taken a much shorter time than it actually did.

And also, one has less patience in one's late thirties, by which time any violent change created by oneself no longer comes from the subconscious but often from mere irritation at the boredom and slowness of life. Even a marxist-revolutionary is in the grip of the bourgoise imperialist ethos from which he came. In fact for many people from the middle class, taking up the cause of marxist revolution is only another form of imperialism, though I am not suggesting this was so with Guevara.

With the score or so men at his disposal, his effect in Bolivia was nevertheless great. Almost all the best troops of the Bolivian army, and its United States advisers in counter-insurgency warfare, took part in a campaign to suppress his activities, and they suffered many casualties before achieving this. Guevara was captured and then killed in October 1967.

The 'foco' which seemed to fit so well in theory turned out to be essentially unworkable. The theory mixes well with the temperament of the South American middle-class communist revolutionary, and no doubt in practice it is still going on in modified form, but other and more patient methods are needed to turn the peasant against those who seek to keep him docile and slavish.

Yet Guevara's ideas were never basically wrong. Because he chose an unsatisfactory place and was defeated does not mean that his ideals and qualities won't win in the end. He was not destined to strike up a spectacular Dien Bien Phu in South America and grow renowned as a general with the fame and long life of Nguyen Giap in North Vietnam.

Heroes, theoreticians, martyrs and leaders will come as they are needed in the tormented continent of South America, and 'Che' Guevara had some of all these qualities rolled into his wide personality. His ideas were young ideas. He could not bear to grow old. He did not have it in him to 'form a government' after the shooting was over—and who can blame him? His various jobs as minister in the post-revolutionary Cuban government were not, one suspects, the happiest of his life. One must applaud him for wanting to make revolutions rather than governments, governments which in most cases distort history into pageants of inhuman clockwork action.

From the evidence one can deduce much. Guevara, though a constant victim of his illness, had a great idea to sustain his body through immense hardship. Life in the jungle has the most devastating effect on the physical system. To survive a week is to survive a lifetime. But a body can live on ideas, though the man must be of an extreme toughness and be absolutely human at the same time. A fanatic would not survive.

In spite of all the information I received about his life I did not find enough material to base a film on. No one book existed for my purpose, so I had to read a great many subsidiary volumes which treated of him only briefly, as well as scores of articles and interviews in French and Spanish which began to appear immediately after his death. Everyone seemed to have been at school with him, though no one—it appeared to me—was in retrospect able to get at the essential 'Che'.

Where was the bridge between the idealist and the ordinary fearing and feeling man out of which great ideals are born? A man can see injustice and not be moved by it. Another sees it, and wants to find a remedy for the unfortunates who suffer under it. One man reacts and the other does not because they are not the same person. It is an easy answer, but the vital question remains, and in every case the answer varies greatly because all people are different. If they are eventually united to try and solve the problem of their country or the world they pool their common aims. Each separate subconscious is put into abeyance so that a greater common consciousness can unite in action. The coalescence of these aims may only achieve success when certain historical and economic conditions arise at the same time, but people must always keep themselves alert and train for them when they do.

With these thoughts in mind I finished the film script, and hoped I was as close to a life of 'Che' as it was possible to get with the information then available. The film was never made, due to many circumstances, and the script rests in the archives of Woodfall Films.

In some ways I am glad it wasn't made. It was too early for such a project. The book that gave the essential spirit of 'Che' Guevara had not yet appeared.

Now I think it has. When Hilda Gadea's book was shown to me in typescript I knew that here was the 'Che' Guevara of real life— the husband, student, traveller, father, lover, and last but not least, communist revolutionary.

Hilda Gadea tells of her first meeting with 'Che' Guevara in Guatemala, and all that subsequently happened to them in Mexico. The story ends with Guevara setting out on the motor vessel 'Granma' with the Cuban revolutionaries for the coast of Cuba— though the rest of his life is sketched in, for that was not the last she was to see of him.

Her story is told in simple, forthright language with no pretence at literary style, and Guevara's life stands out not only as that of a great man, but also as an ordinary man. And this is important, because great men with the hearts of ordinary men live longer in the imaginations of peoples than the historical idols that are put into school text-books. Guevara believed in equality, that there shall be neither rich nor poor, oppressors nor oppressed, but one socialist humanity for the whole earth. There is no finer ideal than that, nothing more human to strive and fight for—in spite of its tragic and catastrophic failures so far. Hilda Gadea's book shows that the man who tried, and died for it, was as ordinary as the rest of us who also want it.

She makes this apparent only through absolute honesty and simplicity, as well as intimate knowledge and respect. As the story is told one realises that her pen is accomplishing this difficult task with an ease which makes Guevara into a real person as well as an idealist.

He was guided in most of his actions by a noble heart, and though many of his pronouncements were misguided in the attempt to make everything he thought fall too neatly into a pattern, it may well be that only the best things about him will be remembered.

Lawrence and District

'I have no allocated place in the world of things, I do not belong to Beldover (Eastwood) nor to Nottingham nor to England nor to this world, but they none of them exist, I am trammelled and entangled in them, but they are all unreal. I must break out of it, like a nut from its shell which is an unreality.'

This is what Lawrence might have directly said, words he gave instead to his great heroine Ursula Brangwen at the end of *The Rainbow*. And if one may put those thoughts on to him, and square them with his actions, as I think one can, then he did indeed break out of Eastwood and district, going far beyond that 'dry, brittle corruption spreading over the face of the land'.

His mother died of cancer in 1910 when he was twenty-five years old:

> 'The sun was immense and rosy
> Must have sunk and become extinct
> The night you closed your eyes forever against me.'

The road was clear for him: he jettisoned the sweetheart of his youth, Jessie Chambers, which was a painful and laborious process, and went off with Frieda the professor's wife. Eastwood was finished, rubbed away like the chalked cyphers from a schoolteacher's blackboard. Or so one might have thought. Like many English provincial writers, he did not 'like it here'. His impulse was to get away, to strike out with the only equipment readily to hand, a woman. And the woman he chose (or who was chosen for him) latched on to the only equipment to hand in order to get out of a deadly and failed marriage: another man. Lawrence took his first love (that is to say: his mother) from his father. He took his last

128

love from her husband. And if, as some say, it was these two women who chose him, then one might add that he was the sort of man who had to be 'chosen'. The second vital choosing was simply a logical follow-up from the first.

At any rate, Eastwood was dead—long live the world. Nottinghamshire fell into its dark and deserved oblivion—long live the sun. Who did he leave behind? A father he had been brought up to loathe, and whom he would have disliked in any case. The father was a living example of what Lawrence knew he himself might easily have become. He also saw that much of the father still existed in him, under the writer's clever and protecting skin.

Lawrence left behind his brothers and sisters, and some friends. When he went back, as he did from time to time, it was a dying landscape he visited as far as his spiritual middle was concerned, for it had little charm or reality for him after his mother had died and his youth was laid waste. One has to ruin youth in order to get rid of it effectively, and a writer does it through his novels.

From then on youth and Eastwood existed only in his writing. He screwed it out of his memory and pulled it from his soul so as to put it into his novels and stories, and to have it with him for always, but buried deep enough so that it no longer tormented him. The more he wrote about it the more its attraction died. Not only did *he* leave it, but he used the same departure theme in many of his novels as well. Alvina Houghton cleared out at the end of *The Lost Girl*, and Aaron Sisson packed it in at the beginning of *Aaron's Rod*. Even at the end of *The White Peacock* the bankrupt farmer was considering a new life in Canada. And we all know that Paul Morel can have no further truck with it after the last lines of *Sons and Lovers*. Gerald, in *Women in Love*, finds his final snowy womb in the solitude of the Alps.

The fact of not liking it here mattered very much to Lawrence, because through it he took himself to other countries. His brittle, intelligent, hypersensitive, friable shell that he still had to live with accepted other landscapes more in keeping with his changing and developing ideas. And if he came back to Eastwood at all he

129

returned not even as a tourist, but like a health-visitor wondering whether he should call in the corporation stoving-gangs either to disinfect or destroy it.

The longer he was away from Nottinghamshire the more he hated the ugliness of it. Perhaps the emphasis on ugliness increased the longer and more definitively he was away from it as a ploy to defend himself against the charge of having so heartlessly left it and abandoned certain people there who had done so much for him. In his own estimation, Jessie Chambers might have been one of these.

At any rate his preoccupation with its ugliness grew with absence. Plain enough at the end of *The Rainbow*, it goes on through all those novels and stories in which 'The North' appears, until the final maniac rantings of Mellors the gamekeeper in *Lady Chatterley's Lover*. In this last novel he even scorns the young colliers going off to dances in Mansfield on their motorbikes, almost as if they didn't deserve such good fortune and would be much better off knitting Indian blankets under the greenwood tree.

Lawrence loved strong men, except his father, whom he was too close to to regard as strong. But he only ever took notice of women during his life, though nothing can be held against him for that. He was dominated by his mother, guided by Jessie, and driven by Frieda. It may well be that a man of such sensitivity and passionate talent can have few meaningful women in his life.

Another powerful factor was landscape—another sort of love. On his later travels he was infatuated with strong landscapes, grandiose and dangerous scenery. But his true love, and maybe the truest of his life, was that significant and magic circle of which Eastwood was the centre. 'That's the country of my heart,' he said in a long reminiscing letter to Ralph Gardner, written from Florence at the end of 1926. In his various novels and stories the Eastwood locality had many made-up labels: Eastwood, Beldover, Netherthorpe, Woodhouse, or Teversall. He loved the beauties of the area till he died, but what he considered to be the ugliness he increasingly disliked, and fulminated against.

If the region was in any way responsible for some of the rage and choler in him it was perhaps because it was neither totally ugly nor completely beautiful, neither one nor the other but a jumble of ambiguities that found a ready reflection in himself.

It was the scars and still working wounds of industrialisation that gave the Nottinghamshire–Derbyshire border the strength and power which was to release his descriptive genius for those parts of the world where landscape had beauty as well as power. The power of ugliness he early recognised, and maybe it acted as a catalyst for the beauty in him. The best example of this ambivalent stance comes out in his poem 'The North Country':

> 'The air is dark with north and sulphur, the
> grass is a darker green
> And people darkly invested with purple move
> palpable through the scene.'

Much of his unreasonable hatred of the urban and industrial landscape came from the above-mentioned three women, and found fertility in himself. It was an attitude he never let go of. It also fitted in with his own sensitive nature, otherwise it couldn't have got such a grip. It might have been a literary inheritance as well, for it has always been a favourite theme with certain English writers to bewail the ruination of sweet and rural England, on the automatic assumption that towns are hell and villages paradise. It still is, for not only does tradition die hard, but so does a longing for peace and non-involvement.

Lawrence was of course always an 'involved' man, but nonetheless he fitted the isolationist person in that he saw little but deadliness in the spread of nineteenth-century industry. Such views, and the extremity with which he held them, led him to despise people more than was good for him. For this reason his early novels, ending with *The Rainbow*, are the best because he is tender and just to his people, but after that work the stomach and humanity seems to go out of them.

Another factor, and one which has not perhaps yet been properly explored, is that he had to get away from England because of the suffocating class atmosphere existing in Edwardian and Georgian days—which in many ways is still with us. In Italy or Germany or Mexico an Englishman was more likely to be accepted as a 'gentleman', no matter how poor he appeared to be. If his aristocratic wife washed the sheets in their Italian cottage it would be seen merely as a mark of eccentricity.

He also said early on to Jessie Chambers that people would think it silly for a collier's son to write poetry, suggesting that he could not see himself opening fully as a writer among such people and such 'ugliness'. Baring his soul to people so close to him, who were not normally able to expose themselves in this way, obviously appeared too inhibiting a factor to fight against, so sooner or later, some way or other, Lawrence had to put himself at a good distance from it.

I once wrote in an article—perhaps too hastily—that to me Lawrence was inconsistent. Before the age of thirty he was a fine writer, while after it he was something of a crank, apart from odd patches such as the first half of *The Lost Girl*, which was written mostly before he was thirty anyway, though it was not published until 1920. One might also mention the middle section of *Kangaroo*, in which he described the persecution habits of the British nation he was almost called-up to defend. To me though he never seemed much of a prophet or a philosopher, roles which I feel he was pushed into by certain people he came into contact with after he had started out on his travels.

After leaving Eastwood he created his own lyrical backwater of idealised folklore. To begin with he made his way to Catholic parts of the world, went from one to another for the rest of his life. Perhaps if there had been no Reformation in England he would have spent more time at Eastwood. But he had to go to those places where the female spirit of the Virgin Mary was in the ascendant, where mother-worship of the Latins was the norm. Either that or, as in Mexico, it was superimposed on to the Aztec spirit of the sun——a very queer mixture indeed.

By the time of *The Lost Girl*, which was issued after the Great

War, and *Women in Love*, published in 1921, he began to lose his grip on local topography, and in *Lady Chatterley's Lover* it was as if he were writing about a sort of black-dream country that did not seem human or real. But though he'd lost touch with his own native soil he had gained infinitely valuable contact with other areas of his soul. From leaving his own acres behind, no matter what the final motives were, he inherited the wider expanses of the earth. Many readers and erstwhile admirers may not thank him for this, but English literature is richer for it. In one sense, by not liking it here, he gained the world. In another sense he gave us the best of both worlds by leaving Nottinghamshire, even though he left the most generous part of his spirit there.

Lawrence, in fact, was born only a mile from Derbyshire. You walk down the hill of the main road out of Eastwood until you come to the railway station on the right—which is now smashed and boarded up. Then you cross the canal and the meagre Erewash, and you are out of Byron's country. After another dozen miles you approach Matlock and get into the Pennines. The ugliness has gone. Picturesque though at times claustrophobic valleys, and wide open hill-ranges are immediately to hand. There is all the beauty in the world, or enough to satisfy a young man, only half a day's bike ride from Nottingham, and even less from Eastwood. Byron, a frequent visitor to Matlock, said that 'there are things in Derbyshire as noble as Greece or Switzerland', and the Matlocks may indeed remind one of the little valley-resorts of the latter country.

After I was fourteen and bought a bicycle I took that road, sometimes alone, occasionally with others, puffing up out of Nottingham through Aspley and Cinderhill. There is a colliery at this latter place, depicted as Tinder Hill in *Sons and Lovers*. In Lawrence's time a bumpy stretch of road ran through it, over which the injured father of Paul Morel was taken on a cart to the hospital in Nottingham after a pit accident—the subject of that famous dialect poem 'The Collier's Wife'.

Beyond Eastwood Hilltop one free-wheeled down to the

Erewash, which was followed by a sure push-up to Codnor and Ripley, and many another walk with the bicycle before coming into Matlock. At that time, before I'd ever heard of D. H. Lawrence (I didn't 'discover' him till I was twenty-one), I'd go on Easter weekends through Bakewell and Buxton to Chapel-en-le-Frith, and back to Nottingham via Chesterfield and Clay Cross, sleeping in fields or barns by the roadside, or under the lee of those rough stone walls marking off the fields, thinking the hills beautiful and restful, but in no way hating the small hilltop mining towns and settlements when I got back among them. In fact coming from the built-up protection of Nottingham I felt comforted by the frequent appearance of these places. And at Easter the road was often wet, and the wind could be bitter enough, but the real impulse was to wear out the body after a week in a factory, and reach as far a point from Nottingham as a bicycle could go in one weekend.

The marathon run on a single day was to cycle the twenty-five miles to Matlock, climb the Heights of Abraham of several hundred feet, visit the ancient lead workings of the Rutland Cavern, row on the slate-grey Derwent for an hour and get as near as one dare to the weir without going over it or having to be rescued by an irate boatman, then cycle back to Nottingham before darkness set in—usually on a bottle of milk or lemonade and a packet of sandwiches.

The first novel I picked up by Lawrence was *The Rainbow*, and its opening paragraphs electrified me. Up to this time I had not read much anyway, but certainly nothing like this. 'Whenever one of the Brangwens in the fields lifted his head from his work, he saw the church-tower at Ilkeston in the empty sky.' I knew exactly what he was talking about, at least as far as the places were concerned. I'd walked across those fields, and seen the same church-tower. Later on in that novel Tom Brangwen rides on horseback to Matlock, and there encounters the foreigner in the hotel whom he 'loved for his exquisite graciousness, for his tact, and for his ageless, monkey-like self-surety'.

Such ambivalent remarks concerning foreigners were made by Lawrence all his life in his books and letters. Perhaps by marrying one he thought he had a right to them. It was certainly one way of mixing his inbred parochial attitudes with those of the English Edwardian upper-class people he met with after leaving Eastwood without such prejudices being too much noticed.

But the meeting of Brangwen and the foreigner at Matlock (in the George Hotel?) created the change of horizon that led Brangwen to propose to Anna Lensky, widow of a Polish exile who had come to work as a housekeeper at Cossethay (Cossall) vicarage.

Tom Brangwen, the grandfather of Ursula, lived at the nearby Marsh, a mile to the north. Before the Reformation there existed a Benedictine cell or chapel of St Thomas, according to Britton's topographical work on Nottinghamshire which I am sure Lawrence must have read (based, it seems, on Thoroton's *Antiquities*), thereby showing that his first Brangwen was appropriately named.

Cossall and the Marsh is now divided from Nottingham by the M1 motorway, and a whole wood nearby has been uprooted to accommodate a service area. Tom Brangwen, in his later years, drove towards home one wet and stormy night after a drinking bout at the Angel in Nottingham. It is hard to know whether Lawrence had an actual pub in mind because the original and notorious 'Angel' on High Pavement was pulled down in 1849, about half a century earlier.

Brangwen's horse drew him along half asleep through the dark and muddy lane winding by Bilborough and Strelley. When he got home he was drowned in the flood swirling around his farm because the Erewash Canal nearby had burst its embankment during his absence.

Concerning the innumerable places in which an author makes his characters sort out their destinies, and from time to time act on them, it is interesting to track each one down and match it to the fictitious name and few lines of description he gave to each.

Sometimes, with Lawrence, the actual names are used, but often made-up ones, and whether an event is of vital importance or not, it is pure chance or whim which one it is. Many of these places can be traced. Nethermere Valley is the course of a stream called The Dumbles, with steep and wooded hills to the north and south, but covering a smaller actual area than Lawrence's word-pictures suggest—as was often the case with Thomas Hardy, in his landscape descriptions.

The cleft of Nethermere is lush, green and wet in late spring— when I went there recently, approaching it from Annesley. Almost hidden from the road is Strelley Mill, the Felley Mill Farm of *The White Peacock*.

It would be futile to run through the dozens of such examples of topographical identification. One might easily say, after much tramping and crude detective work: 'I am sitting on the exact fence that Ursula Brangwen got over in such fear and panic when the horses chased her, at the end of *The Rainbow*'—but it may not be the place at all because perhaps the writer mingled so many clues that the spot can never be found. Nor would it matter if it could. Or maybe he made it so specific, on the other hand, that it is easy to come across. We don't finally know. It isn't very important. Yet all in all, Lawrence's map of his native habitat and hunting ground was fairly accurate, especially regarding places, as one can see from a one-inch Ordnance Survey map. Opening it from time to time as one goes through the novels one realises that he generally tended to disguise places the closer they were to Eastwood. Further away, it did not matter so much, and he gave real names.

Eastwood was no cut-off mining village, but a thriving community. It was a well-known place in Nottingham, a sort of half-way house through which thousands of people passed to get to Matlock and the Pennines—hikers, cyclists, buses, or people out on mystery trips who might not know where they were going because they'd stopped at so many pubs already they were too sloshed to care or take notice. (Usually of course they knew only too well, for each bus had its ancient traveller who'd been to every place in the county—and many out of it as well, while soldiering or sailoring.)

There were wealthy houses in the neighbourhood of Eastwood, and the area itself was by no means poor. In the nineteenth century Lord Palmerston contributed to the founding of the Mechanics Institute. Coal had already been its richness for centuries. In 1812 Britton, paraphrasing Thoroton no doubt, wrote that 'those who chuse to gossip with the sage chroniclers of the place, will be told a wonderful story of a farmer being swallowed up alive in the parlour of the village alehouse, while he was swallowing a cup of ale, to the great surprise of the host, who by this means discovered that his humble mansion was built on an exhausted coal pit.'

Set by the Erewash Valley it was a special area which also had a southern egress to the Trent, which gave it an opening to the sea and overseas. It was under the influence of various escape routes, set between north and south, east and west. The main line from London to Manchester ran up the Erewash Valley, with a station at Pye Bridge. In *Sons and Lovers* this station is known as Sethley Bridge and it is here that Paul Morel and his sister (Lawrence himself and Ada) went to meet their brother William coming home for a holiday from London.

The train, it being Christmas Eve, was more than two hours late, and they were afraid of the meat at home getting overcooked or cold. They waited in the frost and mist until he came, so that all was forgiven when handsome but ill-fated William, carrying his Gladstone bag, went back with them and burst into the house.

In the same book Paul's mother takes him one afternoon to visit Mrs Leivers, her friend at Willey Farm (Haggs Farm) three miles away. There he meets Miriam the daughter, and his description of their long association makes *Sons and Lovers* the finest novel of adolescent love in the English language.

When he was nineteen Paul went walking with Miriam and other friends to the Hemlock Stone. It made a long day there and back. At this time he was working at Jordan's factory in Nottingham, and earned twenty shillings a week. Lawrence worked a few months in a similar factory (Heywood's, manufacturers of surgical appliances) at the age of fifteen, but his appropriate counterpart in *Sons and Lovers* stayed some three years.

The happy group crossed the railway line and went into Ilkeston— 'a town of idleness and lounging. At Stanton Gate the iron foundry blazed. At Trowel they crossed again from Derbyshire into Nottinghamshire. Crowds of other Easter Friday trippers were at the Hemlock Stone, out for the day from Nottingham. Paul found the stone disappointing: . . . a little, gnarled, twisted stump of rock, something like a decayed mushroom, standing out pathetically on the side of a field.'

Two of the party began to carve their initials on it, 'but Paul desisted, because he had read in the newspaper satirical remarks about initial carvers, who could find no other road to immortality'. The last time I was there I noticed that railings had been put around it.

In Britton's book on Nottinghamshire the Hemlock Stone is more flatteringly described, but maybe it was not so weather-beaten a century earlier: 'Between these hills, on the brow of a rising ground, is a very curious and conspicuous object, called the "Hemlockstone". This is an insulated rugged mass of rock, or reddish sandstone, upwards of thirty feet high, and consisting of very thin *laminae* dipping to the west; its extreme breadth from north to south is about twelve feet at the base, but spreading at about two-thirds of its elevation; and its thickness below is about four feet. In outline, it bears some slight resemblance to a mush-room, and is evidently wearing away, from the effects of the weather.'

Some say that the Hemlock Stone is a pagan relic, some that it is not. Nevertheless it is famous around Nottingham as an excursion and picnic point. The huge rock was surmounted by two broad and distinct masses of a hard-wearing green ragstone, thus giving it the mushroom appearance, called in the vernacular 'hemlock stone'. Perhaps its name derived from the colour of the plant. By some misdirection of primitive logic it was said that to run seven times around the Hemlock Stone was a sure cure for 'the rheu-matics'.

On their return to Eastwood Miriam misses Paul, and goes back along the lane to look for him. He has lagged behind to mend his mother's umbrella which got broken. The effect of the Hemlock Stone on them was said to have been insignificant, but Miriam 'always regarded that sudden coming upon him in the lane as a revelation'. It was the first sign of their relationship deepening into a love that both of them grew afraid of but thought might last for ever because they did not for a time know how to end it.

In those days the Hemlock Stone was a fair way from Notting-ham city, but new houses have now crept up Stapleford Hill immediately behind, and anyone living in them who has rheu-matism can run around it in their dressing gowns before breakfast, if they believe in all that, which I imagine they don't. I often walked to it along the canal from Nottingham, or cycled down the lane from Balloon Houses, finding this route the quietest. But nowadays the lane that Lawrence took back towards Trowel and Eastwood, and where Miriam came upon Paul Morel absorbed in mending his mother's umbrella 'as a revelation' has many new houses on either side, and is no longer so isolated. It might even have been that part of the lane where it bridges the motorway.

A few days later Morel and Miriam went on another holiday excursion, to Wingfield Manor. Again with friends, they got on a train to Alfreton, and visited the church there. 'The place was decorated for Easter. In the front hundreds of white narcissi seemed to be growing. The air was dim and coloured from the windows and thrilled with a subtle scent of lilies and narcissi. In that atmosphere Miriam's soul came to a glow. Paul was afraid of the things he mustn't do; and he was sensitive to the feel of the place. Miriam turned to him. He answered. They were together.'

They went on, to Wingfield Manor, and: 'It was past midday when they climbed the steep path . . .' to one of the finest ruins in Britain. Lawrence had the steady absorbent eye of young genius in these early novels that was never to be surpassed or even matched in later work. He not only had youth and love on his side but, what was just as important, his own land combined and wrapped up in it. It mattered more than one thinks. It mattered perhaps more than he knew at the time. Place is everything—soil in the throat, under the feet, in the hands, the nostrils clouded with soot and pollen, the first smells and sounds of life still immediate. Cold grass bends under the frost in winter. Bracken burns in the summer. Youth is so strong that even the machinery of hope doesn't weigh into the scales in one's zest for life. Life simply *is*. Everything is in unison, tragic fate burning away, with youth coolly observing it while not being able to do much about it. But he who is going to be a writer determines early on to break up that unison in himself. He is set on leaving the place that helped him towards such intensity, because that intensity proves too much for him if he dallies and stays there, or else it dies on him.

If Lawrence hadn't been born in Nottinghamshire he would not have been the same writer. Like all other nations perhaps, England is full of little countries, for better or worse, dozens of little class, race and geographical divisions which fortunately defy analysis or sociology. It still pertains more than is generally admitted, and only writers are properly equipped to chart a way between them to the more fundamental issues that lie beyond. I don't suppose Stendhal would have been the same writer if he hadn't been born in Grenoble; nor Balzac at Tours. But while place is everything, it is also nothing. We are all born on ships at sea as far as our souls are concerned, no matter how solid the earth on to which we will fall and maybe walk as soon as we are let loose to try.

Eastwood was and is a township, and the surrounding country-side, which I know well because I have covered every lane and bridlepath, much of it on foot but also by that greatest invention of all time, the bicycle, from an early age on my forays out of Notting-ham. The nearest point to the city over five hundred feet high is Misk Hill, just beyond Hucknall Torkard church where Byron's tomb is kept. Lawrence's father used to sing in nearby Newstead Abbey choir as a boy.

From the summit of Misk Hill one can look southwest and see
the church spire on the hilltop at Eastwood that Paul and Miriam
gazed back on from Crich Stand at the foot of the Pennines in
Derbyshire when they went to Wingfield Manor. Such roaming
is a constant wonder of triangulation, surveys that fix themselves
in the heart and stay there.

Through Eastwood people flocked to the spas and pleasure-
haunts of the Peak District, but north and south of Eastwood it is
half town and half country, slum and mansion, pitstock and folly,
red brick and priory ruins, lime-kiln and green glen, farm house
and ironworks. It is the mixture that makes a landscape seem so
vast in small mileages, an exploring ground that baffles the mind but
goes far towards opening it.

At thirteen Lawrence won a scholarship to Nottingham High
School. The building always had a forbidding aspect to me when
I passed it along Forest Road. It was not too far from where I
lived, yet in a different sort of district. Often we threw apples over
the wall to show our disapproval of it, on our way back from
scrumping up Woodthorpe Grange.

Lawrence's mother had once been a schoolteacher, and he was
brought up by her to have no such fears and inhibitions. He liked
it and, being an intelligent child, went on to become a student-
teacher at Ilkeston, and then at twenty-one to do botany at Nottingham University College. The present-day university was built at
High Fields near to Beeston, and Lawrence satirised it in his poem:

> 'In Nottingham, that dismal town
> where I went to school and college,
> they've built a new university
> for a new dispensation of knowledge.'

The grounds of the university contain a boating lake and swimming baths, a good place to roam to from the hot streets of Radford
during late spring and summer.

The university is the first bit of Nottingham visible from the
train after coming up from London—on rising land beyond an

evenly spaced line of poplars like a row of candles. The long grey building itself has a slimmish square tower set in the middle. It's a bit like a slab of long cake, not too heavy from a distance, which looks as if it can be enjoyed in various ways.

Examining it intently from the train window every time I pass it by, it occurs to me that there must be a wonderful field of fire over the Trent from the top and southerly-looking windows. The building commands two main roads leading into and out of the city. What's more, the lake acts as an outer defence work, a boating lake in fact which skilfully narrows the approaches to the main building, canalising routes of attack through which the assailants would not have a chance of succeeding.

The university is almost as strong as the Castle which, a mile or so further on, is as ugly and menacing as ever, until one gets to the museum inside, or stands by the southern wall to look over Clifton Grove and Wilford.

In *The White Peacock* Cyril, the narrating hero of the book, went to the Castle with Meg: 'We stood on the high rock in the cool of the day, and watched the sun sloping over the great river-flats where the menial town spread out, and ended, while the river and meadows continued into the distance.' In the Castle Museum the young Paul Morel won first prize in a painting competition, and his picture was exhibited there. Lawrence himself began drawing and painting at an early age, though there is no evidence that he won any such competition.

From the Castle one can see the high wooded escarpment of Clifton beyond the Trent, and Clifton Grove which runs along the top of it, where Henry Kirk White walked and wrote his melancholy odes, before dying of consumption at twenty-one. The wide two-mile Grove goes along the level ridge, between elm, beech and oak trees. Paul Morel in *Sons and Lovers* took Clara there after more or less breaking with his childhood girl-friend Miriam Leivers—who in real life was Jessie Chambers. With Clara he scrambled down through the foliage to the shore of the swiftly running Trent. The bank is so steep that if it were not for the trees impeding progress one might go straight into the water.

They went on to Clifton Village, and 'the old lady at whose house they had tea was roused into gaiety by them'. The cottage is still there, and I remember it well, for it was always a favourite and convenient place to have tea with your girl after a country walk and some courting up the Grove. I daresay it is even now, especially for people from the housing estate which flanks it.

Those whom the gods love die young; but those whom the gods hate stay young. Lawrence, to give up his youth, had to leave Nottinghamshire, as if determined to give the gods no cause to hate him. And yet it had meant too much to him to put up with it any longer. He'd suffered a great deal and had learned enough from it to want to get out. His mother had died of cancer, and he had broken with Jessie Chambers because of her too intense and possessive love. He was, she said, a man who had to have all his decisions made for him, though she had connived in this for a long time, until she sensed that maybe he wasn't her kind of man at all because of it, and that in any case there were finally some decisions over which she could not have any control.

After his time at Nottingham University College he went to London and worked as a teacher. But he was not yet free of his youth. Though there was little to hold him to it, how was he to get away from it? It was almost as if life had eaten him up already, and that he had devoured life so that it should not consume him entirely—a contest of mutual annihilation before breath itself ran out. He needed the first and final change in order to survive, that vital break which would enable him to continue writing about it.

There was little to keep him in Eastwood. He had already published *The White Peacock*, had written *The Trespasser* and was working on *Sons and Lovers*. But though he could do the fictionalised first novel while still on home ground, he could not really square with the autobiographical *Sons and Lovers* until birthplace and youth were some way behind. To translate pain and love into art, one needs to be at a distance, and *Sons and Lovers* was finally finished in Northern Italy.

All that had nurtured and tormented him had to be put beyond the horizon, in every possible way. In 1912 he met Frieda Weekley, the German-born wife of a professor at Nottingham University, and the mother of three children, who was some years older than himself. They not only 'clicked', but went away to Germany, beginning a love-affair which led to her divorce from Weekley and marriage to Lawrence. They stayed together till his death in the south of France in 1930.

At forty-four years of age he was ready for the second great leap of his life. The first one, in his twenties, had carried him far enough, and lifted him out of a phase that his spirit found utterly insupportable. Now, that second phase was spent, and it was time to move on to another life-era.

But life is not a series of little boxes. One cannot reckon without the cost of making the first great break which, in Lawrence's case, robbed him of the life-force to go on into a third, final, and more fruitful part of his life.

Though he travelled over much of the world in the last eighteen years, Nottinghamshire was still to figure in many of his novels and stories. But the local bucolic intensity that filled the first books was lacking in them, while something else took its place.

That famous Last-of-England picture from *The Lost Girl* which typified Lawrence's departure from his own country after the Great War, during which four-year lunacy he had been persecuted for having a German wife, is one of the most suitable to end on:

'For there, behind all the sunshine, was England, England, beyond the water, rising with ash-grey corpse-grey cliffs, and streaks of snow on the downs above. England, like a long ash-grey coffin slowly submerging.'

It sank into Lawrence himself, and rotted in him.

Robert Tressell

The Ragged Trousered Philanthropists is a novel about a group of painters and decorators, and their families, in Mugsborough (Hastings) around the year 1906. It describes the workman's life of that time, the subjection, deception and destitution of the people whose labour helped to create the luxury and glitter of the Edwardian Age. It is the age which those who did not have to live in it still like to refer to as the good old days of pomp and circumstance, the apex of England's greatness, the time before 1914 when everyone knew his place and because of it was supposed to be contented and grateful. Those who had money were not only living off the fat of the land, but off the lean of the people as well.

I read an abridged version of Tressell's book when I was with the air force in Malaya. It was obvious straightaway that the writer, in not calling it 'The Ragged-*Arsed* Philanthropists' had chosen its final and more proper sounding title knowing that otherwise it would not be published.

The book was given to me by a fellow wireless operator from Liverpool, a corporal, who said: 'You ought to read this. Among other things, it's the book that won the '45 election for Labour.'

I didn't know that it had been cut to half its length, but it certainly appeared strangely put together, ending as it did on a note of utter despair, suggesting that cranks who believed in Socialism could do nothing better than think of suicide. The latest paperback edition published by Panther Books, however, in 1965, ends the way the author intended, and gives quite a different impression.

It isn't easy to say precisely what effect the book had on me when I first read it. It certainly had a great one, because it has haunted me ever since. Those whose lives have touched the misery recounted

145

by Robert Tressell can get out of it many things: a bolstering of
class feeling; pure rage; reinforcement of their own self-pity; a
call to action; maybe a good and beneficial dose of all these things
—and perhaps, after all, none of them, because somehow the novel
finally transcends class warfare in its evocation of pure tragedy, for
it is as realistic a description of the human jungle as has ever been
made. Whatever else one says, it is one of the finest of English
novels.

Owen, the main character, tries with marvellous patience and
ingenuity to enlighten his workmates, to tell them how socialism
could level out riches and give them not only a little more to live
on, but also real hope of alleviating their inequalities for good. They
won't listen, so he calls them philanthropists, benefactors in tattered
trousers who willingly hand over the results of their labour to the
employers and the rich. They think it the natural order of things
that the rich should exploit them, that 'gentlemen' are the only
people with a right to govern. This theme is the soul of the novel,
yet a mass of personal detail keeps it a novel and not a tract.

The workmen in the story seem to feel that, without the present
cruel and hierarchical scheme of things within which they suffer,
their own will-to-power and possibility of advancement—of ever
getting out of it—will be taken from them. Even though in their
lowly state this possibility doesn't in fact exist, they want to keep it
as a dream, as a piece of heavenly bread to sustain them in their
suffering while being deprived of but the barest amount of earthly
bread.

Owen even sees this, but knows they are wrong, and that a
higher form of dignity awaits them if only they will *act*. Finally
though, he can't tell them how to act. Perhaps he is almost as
afraid of them as they are of the void that would for a time be
created in their lives if they did act. It is deadlock—a stalemate
which gives the book its fiery electric energy. There is in reality
no way out—except one.

Robert Tressell (born Robert Noonan) was himself one of the
workmen he describes. He wrote the book in his spare time, and

knew exactly what he was talking about. He died of tuberculosis in 1911, when he was forty, and his book was not published until 1914—in an inanely bowdlerised edition. It has gone through many and varied versions since then, and has sold tens of thousands of copies all over the world.

Strange to say, one of my first thoughts after finishing the abridged presentation was: 'This book hasn't been written by a working man'—thereby displaying those symptoms of faithlessness that so outraged Owen. And yet, this was an obvious assumption because the book had in fact been fatally tampered with by publishers and their editors—something which has now been remedied by the appearance of as full a version as it is possible to make.

Fifteen years later, reading *Tressell of Mugsborough* by F. C. Ball (Tressell's dedicated and indefatigable biographer, and a good novelist himself) I found the following sentence from a letter written by a relation of Tressell's: 'I have told you quite truthfully that Robert was *not* born into the working class. He would have had a very much happier life, no doubt, had he been.'

It is useless to argue about what 'class' a man was born into, but it is interesting to know that Tressell was a person grafted on to working-class life through family misfortune. Little is known about his early years, but one account says that his father was an inspector in the Royal Irish Constabulary.

F. C. Ball has, since 1958, written another (1974) and much fuller biography of Tressell which, apart from being the only one, deserves to be read because it gives an accurate and highly readable account of the life of this neglected writer. It shows how, with great talent and outstanding passion, Tressell grieved for the people around him, for their poverty as well as his own. Add to that his Irish descent and a justifiable detestation of much English callousness and hypocrisy, and also the fact that he was a sick man most of his life, and you have the author of what has become an English classic.

This was the first good novel of English working-class life. A generation before had appeared those works of Arthur Morrison, who wrote *A Child of the Jago* and *Tales of Mean Streets*. Morrison's writing, however, was often as slick as the Sunday newspapers and, though his stories were deservedly popular, he wrote from too far outside his characters. Robert Tressell, on the other hand, put his ordinary people into correct perspective by relating them to society as a whole.

Many working people familiar with Tressell's book talk about its characters as if they knew them, recount incidents from it as if they had happened to themselves only the other day. It is hard to forget such people as Crass the chargehand, Misery the foreman, Rushton the firm's director, and Owen the 'socialist' workman, as well as the women and children who suffer the most. What makes Tressell's book unique is the author's sense of humour and sense of honour. You can laugh at the way tragic things are told, while being led through the fire, only to weep when cold blasts greet you at the other end. He is utterly unsentimental.

The Ragged Trousered Philanthropists has as its theme the class war. This reduces it to a great simplicity, yet also elevates it into tragedy. I have heard it said that working people are not worth writing about because they have few refinements of perceptions, that lack of intelligence denies them expression, and that people who can't express themselves are not good enough material for the novelist. This may be so if the novelist has neither sympathy nor imagination nor knowledge. Self-expression denied to participants in Greek drama gave rise to tragedy of mythic dimensions.

Critics and reviewers often refer to such novels as 'the kitchen-sink school' with contempt, and to their authors as 'the dark people' with derision or fear, and pontificate so glibly on the 'angry young men'; but how much more basic can you get than the problems of the poor? The poor will never be forgiven for not having the same 'civilised' values—but if they did have them perhaps those who criticise them now would be in their place instead. Such critics are, in any case, the people against whom Owen fulminates so ardently—so why should they condescend to be interested in him and his ilk, and ever admit that his poor folk could be the right material for 'art'? Their ivory tower is stuck up England's arse for ever, it seems. It is those who have the money who tell us what art is—or what it is not. Certainly, a great writer like Fielding would have recognised *The Ragged Trousered Philanthropists* as the artistic success that it is.

On its simplest level, a failure to get bread means death, and this conflict goes back even beyond the emergence of tragedy and myth. The attempt to get more than bread—that is, the self-respect and dignity of spiritual bread—is a theme that can emulate myth while still containing the seeds of tragedy or failure.

There is more tragic material in the inability to get bread than in the temporary lapse of morality that shapes the climaxes of most modern novels. There is a greater meaning in the fight to get a more equitable share of bread than there is in the scramble to get more out of a kind of life already at the end of its spiritual tether.

Robert Tressell's workmen either had no class feeling, or they regarded themselves as totally inferior. Because they saw no way of getting out of their predicament, they could only say 'It's not for the likes of us.' If they thought of improving their lives it was only in ways laid down by their 'betters'. Owen realised that this would solve nothing. The 'not for the likes of us' attitude (still widespread, though not nearly so universal) engendered the poisonous inaction of self-pity, sloth, and stupidity. He saw that they must find the solution from their own hearts—which he feared would not happen until their own hearts had been taken from them. By then it would be too late, because in exchange for more bread they would have relinquished the right to demand anything else. They lived in a jungle. The middle class wouldn't, and perhaps couldn't, help them. Only what the workers take is helpful. What they are given is useless.

In some ways Owen's workmates did want to get out of this jungle, but they needed help, more help than they were willing to accept. A tragedy cannot be written about creatures of the jungle, only about those who try to get out of it—or those who succumb to it knowing that it is possible to transform it. Therefore Owen is the most tragic figure in the book.

What relevance has his novel today? Not a difficult question, for it is simply a good book that ought to be read. It is easy to read, like all journeys through hell. It has its own excitement, harmony, pathos. It is spiked, witty, humorous and instructive. Above all it is deeply bitter, because it is a real hell inhabited by real people, a hell made by one's fellow men because they were human also and didn't want to know any better.

The soul of Robert Tressell, in its complete rejection of middle-class values, seems forged in the formative years of the English working class, during the Industrial Revolution of 1790–1832. Tressell no doubt inherited this feeling from his early days as a more independent workman in South Africa. The working people in his time did not have the same clarity, violent outlook, nor intellectual guidance of those earlier men of the Industrial Revolution. Never before or since were they so spiritless or depressed.

England was stagnating, eddying in a cultural and material backwater of self-satisfaction and callous indifference, in which those who 'had' hoped it would go on for ever, and those who 'had not' were beginning to curse the day they were born. This is stated implicitly through Owen's thoughts late in the book: 'In every country, myriads of armed men were waiting for their masters to give them the signal to fall upon and rend each other like wild beasts. All around was a state of dreadful anarchy: abundant riches, luxury, vice, hypocrisy, poverty, starvation, and crime. Men literally fighting with each other for the privilege of working for their bread, and little children crying with hunger and cold and slowly perishing of want.'

The poverty and struggles of the winter so convincingly and realistically described remind me of nothing less than the conditions in the Warsaw ghetto when the Germans were deliberately causing its Jewish inhabitants to die by keeping all provisions from them.

By the time this first great English novel about the class war was published, the power of those who might act was being cut down

on the Western Front. The Great War drained off the surplus
blood of unemployment, and definite unrest. It proved once more
the maxim that war is the father of a certain kind of progress—in
certain societies. I imagine also that Robert Tressell's destitute
workers welcomed it, for a while. They finally died 'tearing the
guts out of the German army' on the Somme and at Passchendaele.

Mountains and Caverns

'Are the duties of the historians of hearts and souls inferior to those of the historians of external facts? Can we believe that Dante has less to say than Machiavelli? Is the lower part of civilisation, because it is deeper and more gloomy, less important than the upper? Do we know the mountain thoroughly if we do not know the caverns?'

On second thoughts perhaps I skipped that passage in *Les Misèrables* when I first read it as a child, rather than face the ignominy of not understanding it. More to my taste would have been: 'Ships and barricades are the only two battlefields from which escape is impossible.' And so is life itself. But I read the book again and again in the next ten years, till most of it was fixed firmly in.

There was a public library less than a quarter of a mile from where we lived. The first time I went I was quietly pleased to note so many books that I could borrow three at a time for fourteen days. I stood just inside the barrier, and for a moment or two, till I became embarrassed at standing still too long in that exposed position, didn't quite know which of the racks and stacks to look in first.

Classified as a child, I could only get at baby stuff, William books, works by Conan Doyle, Rider Haggard, John Buchan. I gluttonously read my way from Montezuma's Daughter to the flat on Baker Street (both equally remote), and then asked the librarian if I could move into the grown-ups' section.

But when he said yes, I went back to reading Victor Hugo, because *Les Misèrables* and *The Man Who Laughed* and *The Hunchback of Notre Dame* and *The Toilers of the Sea* were closer to me than those afore-mentioned sub-classics of the English post-1870 Education Act literature. And rather than persist with Dickens, who for some reason I couldn't stand, I read books of travel (such as *France*

On Ten Pounds) and books of instruction on how to write articles and stories, as well as histories, geography books, dictionaries—anything—apart from Hugo, with Dumas occasionally thrown in. A teacher at school, whose name was Charles Rowe (we called him Percy), saw my interest in geography and politics and lent me G. D. H. Cole's *Social History of Post War Europe*, a book beyond me at the time, though I appreciated his gesture.

I think *books* influenced me more than any title. I was entranced by the volume as an object, stiff covers between which were several hundred pages of magical symbols called *print*. I could flip them and cause a breeze against my cheek, thus demonstrating certain principles of physics. I could make a stack and see them from a few feet away as a pyramid of print, a Pennine of pages. They appeared to me as stepping stones to some state that I didn't yet know about.

Books were plentiful. They were cheap. In Frank Wore's second-hand shop downtown was a cellar with a vast table laden with threepenny volumes, and once the war started and there was more money I could afford at least one or two a week. In that cellar, where a coal fire burned on Saturday afternoons, and the smell of damp books and soot was so intense that I can still remember it clearly, no literary classic was beyond my reach. Yet I still preferred text-books, crumbling lexicons, out-of-date one-volume encyclopaedias, old sixpenny cycling maps, Baedeker guidebooks—anything but fiction. I bought an immense leatherbound copy of the *Book of Job* in French, and read a few pages of that.

I hoarded books, and they caused a certain amount of resentment when I brought them into the house, especially from my father who thought I should spend my cash on something more worth while, such as food or shoes.

But with books I could cut myself off from everybody. I had a refuge—which my parents, brothers and sisters chose not to share or take advantage of. If they wanted to escape they were stuck to the mains wireless. I had only to walk away with a book in my hand.

Books took up space. They were intimidating. If you couldn't read, they were no good to you, so you wanted to kick them aside or sweep them off the table. When you did read, you went on reading, and the more you were absorbed, the quicker you got at the core of the books. The more you read, the more you wanted to read. Reading was mixed with the cinema, *Comic Cuts*, and the *Radio Times*.

I once saw a pyramid of hundreds of dictionaries outside the school stokehole waiting to be incinerated. With a friend I climbed over the high wall during one summer holiday when the place was deserted but for the caretaker, and saw this heap of redundant books. We couldn't understand why they had not been given out free, for all of us to take home. Admitted, most were in bad condition, but there was much use in them still. Along the wall, where they were waiting to be burned, it said in neatly painted white letters: Cleanliness is Next to Godliness—as if the world would be cleaner when fire had polished off these valuable books of words. We descended from our perch and thieved as many good copies as we could carry away.

The Second World War came and went, and I still read only text-books, and books about the war itself. It is almost true to say that I read nothing that was adult till I was twenty. My teens were passed on other matters. After work in the factory I studied navigation, mathematics and meteorology, as an air cadet. Then there was the usual adolescent roistering to pass any spare time that remained.

In Malaya with the RAF, I was stuck for long hours to a radio-set, so there was time to read. I'd brought in my kitbag from England a copy of *The Old Testament*. I met others who also read. A corporal threw me a copy of *The Ragged Trousered Philanthropists* after a long conversation about politics.

I picked up a volume which contained *Sevastopol* and *The Kreutzer Sonata* by Tolstoy in the camp library, and on the troopship I read *A Room With a View* by E. M. Forster, and *The Mutiny on the Elsinore* by Jack London. The fact that I remember the names of these books shows not only that they were 'memorable' in their content, but that it was rare for me to read a book at all.

At best it was random reading, and I couldn't much tell the difference between those books and *The Further Adventures of Jack the Ripper*—though the harder the book was (that is to say, the slower I was forced to read) the more I was aware that I was getting something out of it. Certainly, those early books were unforgettable in the density they seemed to possess.

When I got back to England at twenty, and had to go into hospital with tuberculosis, the real reading started. You name it, I read it—in the following few years. One book I latched on to in hospital was *The Forest Giant* by Adrien le Corbeau, translated by T. E. Lawrence, and published by Jonathan Cape in the twenties. It was a slim book with rather nice woodcuts, a simple story of the birth and death of a tree by a river bank on the edge of a forest. It began as a minute seed falling from a mature parent and being washed down the river. Eventually it lodged on the bank and put out roots, and grew into an enormous 'forest giant' when the course of the river shifted. The book describes its life until, as a dying tree it falls into the dust and bracken.

The book was speckled with 'meaningful' sentences, such as (if I remember correctly: I wrote many down at the time but have lost the notebook): 'An incurable illness is a premature old age, and premature old age is an incurable illness.' Being, as far as I knew, incurably ill at the time, the sentence seemed profound and real. Maybe such a quotation is a bad example, however, and appears rather banal now, but that sort of writing was new to me, and somehow satisfying. It was like going back to a well of pure water I'd inadvertently strayed from.

I've looked for *The Forest Giant* in bookshops, libraries, and houses, but haven't found it. I'd be interested to read it again so as to see what attracted me to it, because it might indicate what my fluid half-formed biological mind was like at that time.

It is no use compiling a list of books I enjoyed. There are too many—and they wouldn't necessarily be the ones that influenced me. Those I liked obviously took me on an escape route away from one reality, but into another that seemed to enlarge my spirit because it allowed me to get a proper grip on my dreams. So I can mention *Nostromo, The Charterhouse of Parma, Moby Dick, Tom Jones, Wuthering Heights, Tess of the D'Urbervilles.*

Those books that influenced me are the fundamental texts that hit me, sank so deeply I hardly felt their hidden purpose at the time. Or, what was also true, they stayed with me—or comforted me— at a time of crisis. It's not often possible to say which books these were, because what I read in them only takes effect many years after the crisis, rising up suddenly out of memory when I am not thinking about them, or when another hard knock is imminent.

While *Les Misèrables* took me through the prolonged crisis of childhood, *The Forest Giant* helped me to manage the shock of my first illness when I thought I was going to die at twenty: I didn't care to go on living in a state of premature decrepitude. I recovered, as one might know, though it took nearly ten years, and I did it simply by ignoring the fact that I was ill—which is another kind of story.

In both cases I turned to a book and not to people, which must have some significance. The gift of literacy, and the universal accessibility of books, made a priest unnecessary. A self-educated sceptic is fairly independent in that respect.

Since I saw the devastating and healing importance of books it's not so strange that I decided to write one of my own. I looked for those that lent me their eyes, and allowed me to see things in the particular direction my mind and myself had always wanted to take—books that not only showed me how to write, but which inspired me to write in a clear and comprehensible manner.

I won't go too much into that, because this is about reading, not writing—though I've never known how to keep the two separate. Writing fed on reading at first, till I could more or less see the mechanics of it. Then the writing fed on imagination and, last of all, on life itself—a meandering that finally brought the head back to the tail. But it was a long training of ten years, from the age of twenty to nearly thirty—though I don't suppose this is so long when, as Robert Graves states in *The White Goddess*, a Druid-poet went through a twenty-one year apprenticeship.

During the middle part of that decade I came across *Sand*, a forty-page work by Israel Joshua Singer—the best of many gems in a fat and priceless paperback-anthology of Yiddish stories. It is a simple tale of poor but religious people. They are also rough, primitive and quarrelsome: 'After all, a human being is a human being and does human things,' as one of the characters in it is forced to say.

We are taken through all the seasons of an isolated bone-poor settlement on the banks of the Vistula called Podgurna, and I shall always remember the description of the Russian artillery at the nearby fortress firing at the jammed ice-floes in spring, breaking them up so as to save villages from inundation—for which the inhabitants of Podgurna are touchingly grateful.

Reb Jonah, 'the elected rabbi and teacher and beadle and guide of Podgurna' had been taken off as a young man for twenty-five years' servitude in the Tsar's army, and in spite of all the indignities did not give up his religious beliefs. He fought bravely at Sevastopol and gained three medals. He was discharged in Siberia, and spent some years officiating at a village synagogue there. As an old man and a widower he comes back with his daughter Mashka to Podgurna, where he was born—in the Jewish Pale of Settlement.

When the people of the neighbouring and more important village of Grobitze make harsh conditions for Podgurna about coming to worship in its synagogue and using the burial ground, the Podgurna people prevail on Reb Jonah to become their rabbi, so that they can then be independent of the richer and snootier village.

This he does, though in a rather makeshift, inefficient fashion regarding the tighter points of doctrine. He also runs the *cheder* (school) to teach the children Hebrew, and marches them into and out of his classroom like the old soldier he is.

Aaron, the travelling ritual slaughterer, recently widowed, comes by from Grobitze, and is put up at Reb Jonah's house. He is well-

versed in the order of feast-days and ritual, so Reb Jonah is glad
to have him nearby to refresh his own hazy mind. Mashka, the
daughter, serves Aaron with his food, and he gets into her bed one
night, so that trouble really erupts when the women discover she
is pregnant.

They don't find out till after she's given birth, in fact, and they
panic at the disgrace, horrified at what the self-righteous inhabitants
of Grobitze will say. They flow into the humble synagogue of
Podgurna during a service conducted by Mashka's as yet unknowing
pious grandfather. But Pesach Plotnik, the community strongman,
brings his meaty fist down on the pulpit and roars: 'Women and
children, out of here! All of you, you bastards!'

Later he leads a foray against the neighbouring Grobitze, to
forcibly bring Aaron back, who is made to marry Reb Jonah's
daughter. At the wedding-feast you know that the young couple
are going to be as happy as any married pair will be after a few
years together. All has ended well, but it needed a whole community
to put things right.

The story is much more than this bare outline, for it gets more of
life in it than most novels contain. It is the jewel of Israel Joshua
Singer's art—and I afterwards read all his novels and stories, as
well as those of his brother Isaac Bashevis Singer. Together they
have erected a permanent monument to a great but (I'm grieved
to say) vanished culture.

Strange as it may seem—though it never did to me—I felt a
strong connection between the people in these Yiddish stories and
those among whom I'd grown up in Nottingham. Though the
novels I wrote during my stay in France and Majorca bore little
relation to everyday life as I had lived it, my short stories did. They
were set in Nottingham and concerned people I had known, or
characters out of my imagination mixed in with the same realistic
background.

I feel that if I had not read *Sand* I should not have written *The
Loneliness of the Long Distance Runner* four years later, or *The*

Ragman's Daugher, or *Mimic*. My stories would not have taken the *form* they did. *Sand* shows that much can happen between A and Z, that a tale is all the better—and richer—for being told in an unhurried, meandering and human way. Not sentimental, but moving and respectful of life. A man should live, if only to satisfy his curiosity.

Sand, a tale I picked at random, led me back and forth through the Yiddish anthology, to read *Kola Street*, *Repentance*, *White Chalah*, *Competitors*—and all the rest—and from them I saw that the historians of hearts and souls were not indeed inferior to those recorders of external facts. The two conditions met in these tales, and though I already knew that such was possible I was happy to find these fine examples of it.

A good time for reading a rich and stylish story is while on a train travelling alone. With strangers round about, and unfamiliar scenery passing the window (at which you glance now and again) the endearing and convoluted life coming out of the pages possesses its own peculiar and imprinting effects. An author has you firmly in his grip when his tale puts the rhythmically beating train wheel, out of your mind. A good book, an absorbing story, stops time, gives further distance to eyes that look inwards. And the greater distance in, the greater distance out.

I felt I had met many of those people from *Sand* before, both in literature and life. Literature belongs to the world, not to one country, and the story was like a country I had once lived in. I don't know why. The people are poor. They are vivid. They feel much. What's more, the author who wrote about their folly and suffering loved them.

People do not live in classes and masses, nations or groups. They are all of them individuals. When I see a long stretch of sand along a sea shore or river bank I know that not one grain is the same as any other, even though there are more than anybody can count.

I place *Sand* with a few other great short stories, and make the following list to show what I mean:

Sand by Israel Joshua Singer.
A Gentleman from San Francisco by Ivan Bunin.
The Heart of Darkness by Joseph Conrad.
Lenz by Georg Buechner.
Las Encantadas by Herman Melville.
The Steppe by Anton Chekhov.
The Sport of Destiny by Schiller.

If I had them in one volume I would place it beside *Les Misèrables* and *The Old Testament*, and row them to my desert island.

I'll also mention *The Anatomy of Melancholy*, by Robert Burton, a seventeenth century priest endlessly expatiating on sin, concupiscence, plague, illness, ghosts, servitude, hypochondria, passion, love, madness, melancholy, medicine, superstition, despair, lycanthropy and jealousy—drawing in hundreds of obscure authors and classical quotations, and linking them in the richest of English commentaries—witty, profound, often misanthropic, but always creating a treasure-house of rare words, original compounds, and far-out anecdotes. It is the sort of packed marvellous idiosyncratic prose that can quench anyone's thirst in the desert of life.

So I stake my heart on that book as well, throw it in the boat to that hypothetical desert island even if it sinks it.

Such books make me, at certain times, happy to be alive, and glad to be a writer. I feel a sense of gratitude when I read those books again that helped me to know for sure who I was and what I wanted to do, books that were opening a door which I knew to exist, but did not have the key to till then, and which led me to the mysteries of the mountains and caverns.